Faith and Life Series Family Guide
Volume 2

Faith and Life Series

Family Guide
Volume 2
Grades 5 – 8

Ignatius Press, San Francisco
Catholics United for the Faith, Steubenville, Ohio

Nihil Obstat: Reverend James M Dunfee
               Censor Librorum
Imprimatur: Reverend Monsignor Kurt H. Kemo
               Diocesan Administrator of Steubenville

© 2012 Catholics United for the Faith, Inc.
All rights reserved
ISBN 978-1-58617-729-4
Manufactured by Friesens Corporation
Manufactured in Altona, MB, Canada in July 2012
Job # 75423
in compliance with the Consumer Protection Safety Act ∞

Contents

Introduction

A Note to Parents

As a parent, you give your child countless good gifts: your love, your time, a home, a family, an education, food, clothing, and daily experiences of joy. The first and greatest of these gifts, of course, is your love.

Through your love for your child—through the sacrifices you make, the affection you show, and the discipline you enforce—you teach him what it means to be a human person: that we are called to live in relation with others, to give our lives away in love for others, and to use our minds and hearts to serve others.

You also, in all those ways, teach your child about God. The love you show your child is his first introduction to a God Who is Love. Likewise the care you provide for him is a living model of the care God provides for all His children.

Your Child's First and Greatest Teacher

Accordingly, because you are your child's first teacher in love, there is no one better equipped than you to be his first teacher in the Faith. More than any teacher, priest, or religious sister, you are uniquely suited to handing on to your child the most important lessons he needs to learn: who he is, why he was made, how he is to live, and for what he is eternally destined.

Indeed, the Catholic Church has made this clear again and again, noting in documents such as *Gravissimum Educationis* that parents are the primary educators of their children, the ones who bear the greatest responsibility in the moral, spiritual, and intellectual formation of their children.

Ever since your child was born and baptized into the Faith, you have been carrying out this duty in countless ways. From teaching him to share with others to taking him to Mass on Sundays, you have been forming his heart and mind in accordance with truth.

Now that your child has begun formal religious education, it might seem as if your role in his moral and spiritual formation has been supplanted, at least in part, by his teacher. Nothing, however, could be further from the truth.

A Tool for Teaching

Religious education is not like other subjects. That is mostly because it is not a subject. It is a way of understanding the world and living in it. Catholicism is a life, not a class, and therefore, the most important lessons cannot be mastered through lectures and memorization.

In order for your child truly to know and love his Catholic Faith, in order for him to become a good, kind, virtuous adult who knows and lives his life according to God's truth, he needs to see you live the Faith as well. He needs to learn about the Faith from you, and he needs to live it with you.

That means, of course, going to Sunday Mass with his family, but it also means talking with you about what he's learning, hearing stories about the way God has touched your life, and practicing the Faith in countless little ways as your family goes about your daily business.

That is the purpose of this *Family Guide*.

It is, on one level, a tool you can use to help your child review what he has learned in class. But it also provides you with quick, simple activities to reinforce those lessons at home. It provides opportunities for your child to expand upon and deepen his understanding of his lessons in the Faith. Above all, it gives you a reason, every week, to sit down and talk with your child about the most important things in both your lives: your relationship with God and your relationships with others.

No one can form your child in truth and love better than you can. It is the hope of your child's school and the publishers of this handbook that the *Faith and Life Family Guide* will be an invaluable resource to you as you carry out this important work and grow in your own relationship with God.

How to Use This Book

Getting Started

Time and Setting
Each lesson has been designed to take no more than fifteen minutes, so it can easily be done in the evening, before or after dinner.

Where you choose to have this family lesson is up to you. It is helpful, however, to be in a quiet place, away from distractions and the television. This will make it possible for you to talk with minimal interruptions. It will be equally helpful to have nearby a symbol of your Catholic Faith, such as a crucifix, icon, or religious picture.

It is strongly suggested that you look over each lesson in this *Family Guide* before sitting down with your child, especially so that you may have ready any materials for which the session might call. You will also find reviewing the lesson and answering questions easier for you if you have already done the recommended reading from your child's textbook, the Bible, and the *Catechism*.

What You Will Need
To prepare yourself for the family lesson, as well as to conduct the actual sessions, you will need at minimum:
- A Catholic Bible, preferably the Revised Standard Version, Second Catholic Edition;
- A copy of the *Catechism of the Catholic Church* or access to an online version.

Several lessons call for a crucifix or an image of Christ crucified, as well as other small items common in most Catholic homes, such as a Nativity set, an image of the Virgin Mary, and a picture of the Holy Family. Although you can always find images online, you might want to consider purchasing these items if you do not already have them. Not only will they help you as you conduct these lesson review sessions, but they will also serve as a constant source of inspiration for your family in your home.

Conducting Review Sessions

In each lesson there are eight components:

1. Lesson Focus
This section is primarily for you, not your child. It provides a brief overview of what this week's unit has taught your child. It would be best if you read the entire chapter in your child's *Faith and Life* textbook before sitting down with him. That way, you will be more prepared to answer any questions he might have. When this is not possible, however, the Lesson Focus will serve as a brief introduction to the topics you will be covering.

2. References

Like the Lesson Focus, this section is for you. Set in a sidebar, it lists Scripture references and *Catechism* passages that directly address the topics covered. Reading these passages before the family session can increase or refresh your knowledge of the individual teachings, answer questions you might have about the lesson, and prepare you to address questions your child will likely have.

The Scripture references in this section follow standard abbreviations. If you are unfamiliar with the abbreviations used, you will find a list of the books of the Bible and the abbreviations for each either at the front or the back of your Bible. Each Scripture reference in the *Family Guide* directs you to a specific chapter and verse, separated by a colon. For example, if one of the Scripture references is taken from the Book of Genesis, chapter 3, verse 15, it will appear in the References section as Gen 3:15.

Similarly, the references to the *Catechism of the Catholic Church* are to paragraphs, not pages. This allows for consistency between different editions of the *Catechism* and makes it possible to search for specific passages online. So, if the *Catechism* references cited in the *Family Guide* are 323–40, you will need to read paragraphs 323 through 340. In the printed *Catechism*, paragraph numbers are clearly marked in bold print at the top left-hand corner of each paragraph.

3. Begin

Every lesson begins with a short prayer. It is important that you begin with prayer for several reasons. First, it helps you focus your attention, shifting it away from whatever you and your child were doing before the work at hand. Second, it reminds your child that this "homework" is different from other homework: it is sacred work. Finally, it welcomes God into the review session, allowing Him to be present and to guide you as you discuss Him and His teachings. It is recommended, but not required, that you use the simple and short Glory Be prayer. If you have another prayer you wish to use, by all means do so.

After you've prayed, it is suggested that you tell your child a short story or lead him in a simple discussion that serves as an introduction to the particular lesson being discussed. This personalizes the material and helps him see what the lessons he has learned in class have to do with the world outside of school. Again, the book offers a suggestion as to what that story or discussion might be, but if you have a different story that you would like to use, feel free to use it.

Finally, you will read a passage from Scripture that summarizes the core of the week's lesson. You may read it aloud, your child may read it aloud, or you may take turns reading aloud if the passage is long.

If time allows, in addition to reading the Scripture passage, you might want to read the chapter from your child's *Faith and Life* textbook aloud. Although this is not necessary, it will help your child to hear you "teaching" the material and serve as a good refresher for him.

4. Summarize

If your child takes only one thing away from the week's lesson, this one-to-two-sentence summary should be it. It contains the essence, or the heart, of the week's lesson. The *Family Guide* offers an example summary, but you may use your own. After concluding the Scripture reading, simply state the summary, and then move on.

5. Review

Much of the material in this section is drawn from the student textbook, but some questions cover a wider portion of the Church's Tradition, with the intention of deepening your child's knowledge of the lesson's subject matter. The answers to these questions are in italics. Ask your child the question, allow him to attempt an answer, and if he cannot give you one, let him know what the answer is. If he struggles with a particular answer, you might want to go over this section with him a second time, either later in the evening or the next morning before school.

6. Apply

The Catholic Faith is objective, meaning there are right and wrong answers about what the Church teaches. It also, however, is subjective, meaning that we all experience and live out those teachings in unique ways. Faith is personal because the heart of faith is a relationship with Christ. It is important that your child understands this. It is also important that he makes the connection between the objective answers to questions in the Review section and his own life. The questions in this section are designed to help him do that. Answers will vary because they are highly personal. Some answers will come easily to your child. For others, he will need your guidance. Feel free to give that guidance and talk with him more about individual answers.

7. Conclude

The session should end with a brief prayer. Concluding with prayer reminds your child of how special and different this review session with you is and helps him experience the act of talking to God, not just talking about God. Praying with you, his parent, is also important. Children learn how to do almost everything they do by imitating their mothers and fathers, and prayer is no exception. Finally, a concluding prayer offers an opportunity to thank God for giving you this time together and for revealing Himself to you in time, Scripture, and Tradition.

8. Follow up

For most children, the lessons learned in religion classes have little meaning unless they are matched by a lived experience of those lessons. Children need to see their parents, siblings, and trusted friends living the Faith, and they need to be given specific ways to do that themselves. These include prayer, worship, receiving the Sacraments, making small sacrifices, and doing good works for others.

Catholicism is rich with such opportunities. You have at your disposal a long and tested heritage of prayers, devotional practices, and history that can help your child live and understand his Faith.

This final section provides you with just a sliver of that heritage. Each week's lesson features three activities designed to reinforce the overarching lesson of that unit. The activities themselves are quite simple. Some take no more than a minute. Others involve a little more time, but not much planning. Some are prayers. Others are craft activities or research projects. Most can be done at home. You can do one activity each week, or you can do all three.

Although some activities are lesson specific, most have an application beyond the immediate material covered, and you should feel free to continue the activity even after the unit is over. For example, the week your child learns about angels, one of the suggested activities is to learn and pray the Prayer to My Guardian Angel (see Appendix). If you or your child discovers that it is meaningful and helpful for your family to pray this prayer every morning throughout the year, you should continue to pray it. In fact, it is the Church's hope that you will incorporate certain prayers into your daily routine.

Likewise, you should feel free to come up with your own activities that reinforce the particular ends of each lesson. Again, you are the primary educator of your child. You know your child and your family best. This *Family Guide* is intended to be a resource for you as you form your child in faith and love, but it should not be seen as the final word on how you live your Faith in your home.

❉ ❉ ❉

The early elementary school years are such an exciting time for children. Learning is almost always a joy and an adventure for them, and their ability to absorb and understand material is immense. Likewise, at this point in life, children have a natural sense of piety. Small acts of devotion such as lighting a candle in church or kissing a crucifix come easily to them, and even theological concepts that adults spend years pondering are accepted quickly by them.

That is why it is so important that you take advantage of these years, doing everything you can in your home to lay a solid foundation on which God can build. A lifetime of joy, peace, love, hope, and faith begins with learning the lessons these pages contain. They are the key to your child's happiness and well-being as an adult, and they are the key to your family's happiness and well-being right now.

Let this time of religious instruction for your child become an opportunity for your whole family to grow in your relationship with God. See it as a gift, not an obligation. You will be blessed for that now, and your child will be blessed by that for years to come.

Credo: *I Believe*

Grade 5

Be watchful, stand firm in your faith, be courageous, be strong.
1 Corinthians 16:13

Lesson 1

I Believe

Lesson Focus | Faith is a gift from God that enables us to believe in him and the truths he has revealed. Some truths, called mysteries, can never be fully understood, cannot be known without God's revealing them, and cannot be believed without God's gift of faith. There is nothing we do to earn this gift. It is a free gift, which we can choose either to accept or reject. The Creed is a statement of what Catholics believe by faith. It summarizes what has been revealed by Christ and his Apostles, according to the teaching of the Church.

1 | begin

- Pray the Glory Be with your child.
- Ask your child what good gifts God has given him. Ask him how he knows those gifts have come from God.
- Read Hebrews 11:1–3 aloud.

2 | summarize

Summarize this week's lesson for your child:

Example: *You know that all those gifts have come from God because of the gift of faith, the gift that helps you believe all that God has revealed. The Creed summarizes those beliefs.*

3 | review

References

- Student Textbook: Chapter 1, pp. 11–14
- Sacred Scripture: Gen 1—3; Mk 14—16; Lk 1:26–35; Jn 6:40; 20:23; Acts 1:1–11; 2:1–6; 2 Tim 4:1
- *Catechism of the Catholic Church*: 153–65, 185–202, 222–57

Review this week's lesson by asking your child the following questions:
1. What is Faith with a capital F? (*The body of beliefs we hold as Catholics.*)
2. What is faith with a small f? (*A God-given power by which we believe in him and all that he has revealed.*)
3. What is a mystery of faith? (*A divinely revealed truth that can never be fully understood.*)
4. What is the Creed? (*A prayer that expresses the chief truths of the Catholic Faith. When we pray the Creed we profess our belief in the Faith.*)

4 | apply

Help your child apply this week's lesson by asking the following questions:
1. What can you do to keep your faith strong?
2. What should you avoid doing so that you won't risk losing your faith?
3. Who do you know that has a very strong faith? How do you know
   _____'s faith is strong? How would you like to be more like _____?

5 | conclude

- With your child, pray the Our Father (see Appendix).

6 | follow up

During the week, do at least one of the following activities with your child:
1. Memorize Hebrews 1:1.
2. At night, pray the Act of Faith (see Appendix).
3. Online or at the library, learn about one of the early-Christian martyrs
   such as Saint Perpetua or Saint Polycarp. Have your child write and
   illustrate a story about the saint or act out a play with siblings or friends
   about the saint's martyrdom.

*In many and various
ways God spoke of
old to our fathers by
the prophets.*
—Hebrews 1:1

notes

_____

_____

_____

_____

_____

_____

_____

_____

The Blessed Trinity

Lesson Focus | By reason alone, we can know that God exists. Only because God has revealed himself to us, however, can we know that God is a Blessed Trinity—Father, Son, and Holy Spirit, three Divine Persons sharing one nature, all equal, all eternal, and each possessing the perfections of God. This is one of the great mysteries of faith.

1 | begin

- Pray the Glory Be with your child.
- Give your child a puzzle with half of the pieces missing. Ask him to put it together. When he discovers he can't complete the task, explain what the puzzle would have looked like.
- Read John 16:5–15 aloud.

2 | summarize

Summarize this week's lesson for your child:

Example: *Understanding the Blessed Trinity is a little like trying to solve a puzzle with some of the pieces missing. By reason alone we can know God exists, but we wouldn't know he is a Blessed Trinity—three Divine Persons with one nature—if he hadn't revealed it to us. It's a mystery of faith, something we know by faith but will never be able to understand fully.*

References

- Student Textbook: Chapter 2, pp. 15–19

- Sacred Scripture: Is 6:3; Ps 102:25–27; 139; Amos 5:8; Mt 28:19; Mk 1:10–11; Jn 16:5–15; Rev 4:8

- *Catechism of the Catholic Church*: 31–35, 199–202, 206, 234, 238–60, 268–78, 293–95

3 | review

Review this week's lesson by asking your child the following questions:

1. What are some of God's divine attributes? (*1. All holy; 2. Almighty; 3. All knowing; 4. Unchanging; 5. All present.*)
2. Who is the First Person of the Blessed Trinity? (*The Father.*)
3. Who is the Second Person of the Blessed Trinity? (*The Son.*)
4. Who is the Third Person of the Blessed Trinity? (*The Holy Spirit.*)
5. Are all three Persons of the Blessed Trinity God? (*Yes.*)
6. Is there more than one God? (*No.*)
7. Did any Person in the Blessed Trinity exist before the others? (*No.*)

4 | apply

Help your child apply this week's lesson by asking the following questions:

1. If God is all knowing, is there anything about you that he doesn't know? What are some things he knows about you?
2. If God is all merciful, is there any sin you can commit that he can't forgive? What is something for which he has forgiven you?
3. If God is all present, is there any place where you can't talk to him? Name some places where you talk to him. Where else could you talk to him?

5 | conclude

- With your child, pray the Our Father.

6 | follow up

During the week, do at least one of the following activities with your child:

1. Memorize Psalm 139:14.
2. Search online for icons of the Blessed Trinity. Using one of them as a model, help your child draw his own icon, and display it in his room.
3. Help your child write a poem, song, or letter to God, praising him for what he loves most about him.

> *I praise you, for I am wondrously made. Wonderful are your works!*
> —Psalm 139:14

notes

_____

_____

_____

_____

_____

_____

_____

Lesson 3

Creator of Heaven and Earth

Lesson Focus | God is the Creator of heaven and earth. He alone has no creator, no beginning, and no end. As Creator, he loves and cares for his creation. Creation, in turn, witnesses to the truth about its Creator—his existence, goodness, and love. God created the world for the service of man, but man must be a good steward of creation.

1 | begin

- Pray the Glory Be with your child.
- With your child, look out your window. Ask him to point out everything he sees that was created by God.
- Together read Genesis 1 aloud.

2 | summarize

Summarize this week's lesson for your child:
Example: *God is the Creator of heaven and earth. He loves and cares for what he made and wants us to love and care for it too.*

3 | review

Review this week's lesson by asking your child the following questions:
1. What are five things God created? (*Answers will vary: trees, flowers, mountains, rivers, man, stars, etc.*)
2. What are five things that man has made? (*Answers will vary: boats, buildings, cars, airplanes, coffee pots, etc.*)
3. What is a great difference between God's creations and man's inventions? (*God creates out of nothing; man makes things out of materials that already exist.*)
4. Who created God? (*No one. God has always existed. He has no beginning or end.*)
5. Did God create the world out of love? (*Yes.*)
6. Why did God create us? (*So that we might know him and love him.*)
7. What does it mean to be a good steward of creation? (*To care for it and use created things wisely.*)

References

- Student Textbook: Chapter 3, pp. 20–23
- Sacred Scripture: Gen 1:1—2:3; Jn 1:3
- *Catechism of the Catholic Church*: 31–38, 218–21, 279–314, 2415–18

4 | apply

Help your child apply this week's lesson by asking the following questions:

1. What in creation tells us that God is powerful? Loving? Wise?
2. What are some ways you can be a good steward of creation? What should you do? What should you not do?
3. How can you thank God for giving us such a good and beautiful world?

5 | conclude

- With your child, pray the Our Father.

6 | follow up

During the week, do at least one of the following activities with your child:

1. Memorize Genesis 1:31a.
2. At night, as a family, pray Psalm 148, with everyone taking turns to read verses aloud.
3. Go on a nature walk in a local park or in your neighborhood. Have your child bring a sketchbook or a camera and draw or take pictures of created things he sees that remind him of God's love, power, wisdom, etc. Make a collage of those pictures at home.

And God saw everything that he had made, and behold, it was very good. And there was evening and there was morning, a sixth day.
—Genesis 1:31

notes

Realm of the Angels

Lesson Focus | Before God created man, he created the angels, intelligent creatures who are pure spirits. There are nine choirs of angels, and each choir has its task. There are also fallen angels, or devils, who, when tested by God, chose to rebel against him and not to follow him. Just as other angels work to lead men to heaven, fallen angels work to lead men away from God into sin.

1 | begin

- Pray the Glory Be with your child.
- Explain to your child why, when you and your spouse both have to be away from home at the same time, you leave your child with a sitter (e.g., you don't want him to be alone; you want someone to be there to help him, watch out for him, protect him, etc.).
- Read Acts 12:1–11 aloud.

2 | summarize

Summarize this week's lesson for your child:
Example: *Because God is a good Father, he also gives us someone to watch out for us — our guardian angel. Angels are God's messengers, and they help him govern and order creation.*

3 | review

References

- Student Textbook: Chapter 4, pp. 24–27
- Sacred Scripture: Tob 4—12:15; Mt 4:1–11; Lk 1:26–38; 2:20; Acts 12:1–11; Rev 12:7–17
- *Catechism of the Catholic Church*: 328–36, 391–95, 1023–37

Review this week's lesson by asking your child the following questions:
1. Do angels have bodies? (*No, angels are intelligent beings who are pure spirits.*)
2. Are angels people who have died and gone to heaven? (*No, angels were created by God to be his servants and our guardians.*)
3. What are demons or devils? (*Angels who rebelled against God.*)
4. Who are the three archangels mentioned in Scripture? (*Michael, Gabriel, Raphael.*)
5. What does the word *angel* mean? (*Messenger.*)
6. Who is the leader of the fallen angels? (*Satan/Lucifer.*)

4 | apply

Help your child apply this week's lesson by asking the following questions:

1. The bad angels fell because of pride: they didn't want to obey God and thought they knew better than he. Have you ever been proud? When?
2. What good things can your guardian angel help you do? What bad things can he help you avoid doing?
3. Do you ever ask your guardian angel for help? If so, when? In what other situations do you think you could ask for his help?

5 | conclude

- With your child, pray the Our Father.

6 | follow up

During the week, do at least one of the following activities with your child:

1. Memorize Matthew 18:10.
2. In the morning, before school, pray the Prayer to My Guardian Angel (see Appendix).
3. Pick one of the Scripture readings from the References section that tells about the work an angel has done in salvation history, and have your child draw a picture of the event or write a short play about it. (Salvation history is the story of God's loving plan, from the beginning of the world, to make all men and women his children, to form the family of man into a family of God.) Act it out with him, or encourage him to act it out for you with siblings or friends.

See that you do not despise one of these little ones; for I tell you that in heaven their angels always behold the face of my Father who is in heaven.

—Matthew 18:10

notes

_____

_____

_____

_____

_____

_____

_____

Lesson 5

Made in His Image

Lesson Focus | God made man in his image. We image God through our ability to reason, to make choices freely, and to love. Adam and Eve were the first man and woman. When God created them, he filled their souls with grace, a share of his life, so they could live in harmony with each other and creation on earth and live with him forever in heaven.

1 | begin

- Pray the Glory Be with your child.
- Ask your child to tell you how he resembles you or your spouse, or both of you. Does he have your eyes? Nose? Hair? Does he have your mannerisms? Your sense of humor? Your love for cooking, gardening, or something else?
- Read Genesis 1:26–27 aloud.

2 | summarize

Summarize this week's lesson for your child:

Example: *Just as you resemble your father and mother, all men and women resemble our heavenly Father. We were made in his image. That doesn't mean that we look like God, but that, like God, we can think, love, and make choices.*

3 | review

Review this week's lesson by asking your child the following questions:

1. How is man like the angels? (*He can think and love and has free will.*)
2. How is man like the animals? (*He can feel, see, taste, smell, and hear things.*)
3. How is man different from all other creatures? (*He is a creature of both matter and spirit, a body and an immortal soul.*)
4. What is man's great dignity? (*He was created in the image and likeness of God.*)
5. What were the preternatural gifts God gave to Adam and Eve? (*They would never be sick, suffer, or die; their wills were strong; and they understood things more easily and clearly than we do.*)
6. What is the supernatural gift God gives to men? (*Grace.*)

References

- Student Textbook: Chapter 5, pp. 28–30
- Sacred Scripture: Gen 1:1–2:25
- *Catechism of the Catholic Church*: 355–84, 1023–29, 1718–24, 1730–48, 1996–2005

4 | apply

Help your child apply this week's lesson by asking the following questions:

1. One of the ways we image God is through our ability to choose right from wrong. Tell me about a time you used that gift to make a good choice? What about a bad choice?
2. How would your life be different if you had the same gifts as Adam and Eve?
3. Every person has great dignity because every person is made in the image of God. Knowing that, how should you treat everyone you meet?

5 | conclude

- With your child, pray the Our Father.

6 | follow up

During the week, do at least one of the following activities with your child:

1. Memorize Genesis 1:27.
2. As a family, talk about the sin of abortion, and then pray a Rosary for the protection of all life from the moment of conception until natural death.
3. Together, make a list of all the things your child can do because he has a soul. Then make a list of all the things he can do because he has a body. At night, thank God for everything on those lists.

So God created man in his own image, in the image of God he created him; male and female he created them.
—Genesis 1:27

notes

_____

_____

_____

_____

_____

_____

_____

The Fall from Grace

Lesson Focus | Like the angels, Adam and Eve faced a test: would they obey God and love him or would they rebel out of pride? They chose to rebel, losing God's gifts of grace and original holiness and justice. All mankind inherited the effects of Original Sin, including concupiscence—a tendency to sin—and suffering, which God permits but doesn't cause.

1 | begin

- Pray the Glory Be with your child.
- Tell your child about a time you disobeyed your parents and did something dangerous and wrong. Explain the consequences that followed your disobedience and what your parents did to help you understand how wrong your actions were.
- Read Genesis 3:1–15 aloud.

2 | summarize

Summarize this week's lesson for your child:

Example: *Adam and Eve's sin was very bad and so its consequences were very severe. We experience those consequences still: we're all born with Original Sin.*

3 | review

Review this week's lesson by asking your child the following questions:
1. Why was Adam and Eve's sin so bad? (*Because they knew God's goodness fully and understood what the consequences would be. They didn't have weak wills.*)
2. How did their sin change the condition of men? (*Pain, sickness, and death became part of man's condition, and men's wills grew weak and inclined to sin.*)
3. How did their sin change the condition of the world? (*The world lost its natural harmony. Disease and natural disasters are a result of this.*)
4. Does God cause suffering? (*No, but he permits it and is able to bring good out of it.*)
5. What ultimate good did God bring out of Adam and Eve's sin? (*The Second Person of the Blessed Trinity became man to save us and restore our friendship with God.*)

References

- Student Textbook: Chapter 6, pp. 31–34
- Sacred Scripture: Gen 3:1–15
- *Catechism of the Catholic Church*: 55–58, 374–412, 1023–29, 1996–2005, 1730–48

4 | apply

Help your child apply this week's lesson by asking the following questions:

1. Tell me about a time you fought against the temptation to sin and chose to do something good. Why was it so hard to do something good?
2. What can you do every day that will make it easier for you to choose good over evil?
3. Can you think of a way God has used suffering or sadness to help you become a better person? Tell me about it.

5 | conclude

- With your child, pray the Our Father.

6 | follow up

During the week, do at least one of the following activities with your child:

1. Memorize Genesis 3:15.
2. At night, pray the Prayer to Saint Michael (see Appendix).
3. Together, read Ephesians 6:11–18. Make a list of the things Scripture says will help protect us from falling into sin. Have your child draw a picture of a knight whose armor bears those words (e.g., a helmet marked with the word *salvation*), or make armor out of cardboard, and let your child design it and label it according to the Scripture passage.

> *I will put enmity between you and the woman, and between your seed and her seed; he shall bruise your head, and you shall bruise his heel.*
> —Genesis 3:15

notes

_____

_____

_____

_____

_____

_____

_____

The Chosen People

Lesson Focus | Before God could send the promised Savior, he had to prepare a people to receive the Savior, a people who would recognize him when he came and understand his mission. He began this work of preparation with Abraham, our father in faith. He continued it with Abraham's son, Isaac, with Isaac's son, Jacob, and with all the descendants of Jacob's twelve sons, who became the twelve tribes of Israel.

1 | begin

- Pray the Glory Be with your child.
- Show your child a family tree that traces the history of your family back for several generations.
- Read Genesis 12:1–3 aloud.

2 | summarize

Summarize this week's lesson for your child:

Example: *After God had made that promise to Abraham, he began building a family to welcome the promised Savior into the world. God started Jesus' family tree with Abraham.*

3 | review

Review this week's lesson by asking your child the following questions:

1 Why is Abraham our father in faith? (*Because he had great faith and because God made him the father of a holy people from whom our Savior was born.*)
2. What promises did God make to Abraham? (*He would give him many descendants and the Savior would be born from his descendants.*)
3. What prophecy was fulfilled by Jacob's receiving both his brother's birthright and his father's blessing? (*"The older shall serve the younger."*)
4. How was Joseph, Jesus' foster father, like Joseph in the Old Testament? (*God spoke to both in dreams, both went into Egypt to save their families, and just as one Joseph was favored by his father, Jacob, the other was favored by the Father, God.*)

References

- Student Textbook: Chapter 7, pp. 35–37

- Sacred Scripture: Gen 12 – 22; 25:19 – 34; 27:1 – 33:1; 35 – 47

- *Catechism of the Catholic Church*: 51–73, 144–46, 410– 12, 705–6, 2570–72

God promised Abraham as many descendants as there are stars in the sky.

4 | apply

Help your child apply this week's lesson by asking the following questions:

1. Abraham did what God asked him to do because he had great faith. What does God ask you to do? How can your faith help you obey him?
2. Jacob received Esau's birthright and blessing because he valued them and Esau did not. How can you show God that you value the knowledge of him and the faith he has given you, which are part of your birthright as a Catholic?
3. Even though the patriarch Joseph endured much suffering, his faith in God never wavered. How do you think you can keep your faith strong, even when bad things happen?

5 | conclude

- With your child, pray the Our Father.

6 | follow up

During the week, do at least one of the following activities with your child:

1. Memorize Hebrews 12:1.
2. Make a family tree for Jesus, beginning with Abraham. See Matthew 1.
3. Learn about the image of Divine Mercy. Draw a picture of it, with its words "Jesus, I trust in you" at the bottom. As a family, pray the Divine Mercy Chaplet (see Appendix).

> *Therefore, since we are surrounded by so great a cloud of witnesses, let us also lay aside every weight, and sin which clings so closely, and let us run with perseverance the race that is set before us...*
> —Hebrews 12:1

notes

_____

_____

_____

_____

_____

_____

_____

Moses Leads God's People

Lesson Focus | Many years after the descendants of Israel were enslaved by Egypt's pharaoh, God raised up Moses to lead his people out of slavery. It took ten plagues, however, to convince Pharaoh to let the Israelites go. He relented only after the tenth plague took the life of every firstborn Egyptian, including both people and cattle. Even then, however, Pharaoh soon changed his mind and sent an army in pursuit of the Israelites. God destroyed that army in the Red Sea after bringing the Israelites safely across on dry land.

1 | begin

- Pray the Glory Be with your child.
- Tell your child about a time when you discovered part of God's plan for your life (e.g., when you realized you were supposed to marry your spouse, follow a certain career path, have a child, do an act of service, etc.). Explain how you felt and what you did.
- Read Exodus 2:1–10 aloud.

2 | summarize

Summarize this week's lesson for your child:

Example: *God has a plan for everyone, but He had a very special plan for Moses. Moses was saved so that he would be able to lead the Israelites out of slavery and into the Promised Land.*

3 | review

References

- Student Textbook: Chapter 8, pp. 38–42
- Sacred Scripture: Ex 2–13
- *Catechism of the Catholic Church*: 62–64, 128–30, 203–13, 265, 1164, 1334, 2574–77

Review this week's lesson by asking your child the following questions:

1. What happened to Moses after his mother placed him in the Nile? (*Pharaoh's daughter found him.*)
2. Why did Moses flee Egypt to become a shepherd? (*He had killed an Egyptian and feared for his own life.*)
3. Why did Moses ask Pharaoh to let God's people go? (*Because that's what God told him to do when he spoke to Moses from the burning bush.*)
4. What was the first plague God sent upon the Egyptians? (*The Nile turned to blood.*)
5. What did Moses do after God parted the Red Sea for the Israelites? (*Led the people into the desert.*)
6. What sacred meal did the Passover meal foreshadow? (*The Eucharist.*)

The Red Sea.

4 | apply

Help your child apply this week's lesson by asking the following questions:

1. When God first called Moses to lead his people, Moses resisted and argued with God. Why do you think Moses did that?
2. Have you ever not wanted to do what God wanted you to do? When? Why?
3. Pharaoh didn't listen to Moses because he didn't love God or his laws. Through sin, he "hardened his heart" (Ex 8:32). How can you make sure you never harden your heart?

5 | conclude

- With your child, pray the Our Father.

6 | follow up

During the week, do at least one of the following activities with your child:

1. Memorize 1 Thessalonians 5:18.
2. Help your child with an examination of conscience (see Appendix) and go to confession as a family.
3. Help your child draw a picture of what he believes is God's plan for his life (e.g., priesthood, marriage, religious life, a certain job, etc.).

> *Give thanks in all circumstances; for this is the will of God in Christ Jesus for you.*
> —1 Thessalonians 5:18

notes

_____

_____

_____

_____

_____

_____

_____

Lesson 9

The Forming of God's People

Lesson Focus | In the desert, God provided for his people, giving them food, water, and laws to help them love him and worship him rightly. That, however, didn't stop them from rebelling and worshipping a false god. Their rebellion was rooted in a lack of trust. Later, once they had arrived and settled in the Promised Land, they still didn't trust God and demanded a king for their leader. Eventually God raised up two great kings, David and Solomon, who helped Israel become a powerful nation.

1 | begin

- Pray the Glory Be with your child.
- Tell your child about a time when he was very little and refused to do something that he does very well now (e.g., eat his dinner, share with his siblings, pick up his toys, etc.). Explain how you taught him to do what was right and eventually he learned.
- Read 1 Samuel 8 aloud.

2 | summarize

Summarize this week's lesson for your child:

Example: *To prepare his chosen people to welcome the promised Savior, God worked with them, much as I worked with you when you were little, teaching you what to do, disciplining you when you didn't do it, and rewarding you when you did.*

3 | review

Review this week's lesson by asking your child the following questions:
1. What three things did God provide for his people in the desert? (*Manna, quail, water.*)
2. In ancient Israel, what was in the tabernacle? (*The Ark of the Covenant; God's presence.*)
3. What is the tabernacle in a Catholic church? (*It is where Jesus in the Eucharist dwells.*)
4. What are the Ten Commandments? (*See Appendix for full list.*)
5. Name two of Israel's kings. (*David and Solomon.*)

References

- Student Textbook: Chapter 9, pp. 43–45
- Sacred Scripture: Ex 19—34:1; 1 Sam 8—16; 1 Kings 1—3:15; 2 Kings 6—8:21
- *Catechism of the Catholic Church*: 709–10, 1961–64, 1724, 2056–2580

4 | apply

Help your child apply this week's lesson by asking the following questions:

1. Name two things that used to be hard for you to do, but are easy now (e.g., playing basketball, writing in cursive, doing multiplication, etc.). Why is it easy to do those things now?
2. Do you think being good and loving God becomes easier the more you do it? How can you work hard at being good and loving God every day?
3. God took good care of the Israelites in the desert. How does he take care of you?

5 | conclude

- With your child, pray the Our Father.

6 | follow up

During the week, do at least one of the following activities with your child:

1. Memorize 1 Timothy 4:7b–8.
2. During the week, visit the tabernacle in your church. Pray for a few minutes there.
3. Help your child write a description of the type of person he wants to be when he grows up. What virtues does he want to possess? What good does he want to do for others? Talk with him about his description; then help him make a list of things he can do now to start becoming that person. Hang the list and description where he'll see it.

> *Train yourself in godliness; for while bodily training is of some value, godliness is of value in every way, as it holds promise for the present life and also for the life to come.*
> —1 Timothy 4:7-8

notes

_____

_____

_____

_____

_____

_____

_____

Lesson 10

The Words of the Prophets

Lesson Focus | Before the Savior came, God spoke to the Israelites through the prophets. The prophets reminded people of God's laws, called them to repentance when they broke them, and kept them mindful of their covenant with God. For this the prophets were often hated, even killed. Isaiah and Jeremiah were two of the most important prophets in ancient Israel. The last and greatest prophet of the Old Testament was John the Baptist.

1 | begin

- Pray the Glory Be with your child.
- Tell your child about a time you were doing something wrong and someone had to remind you of the right thing to do. Was it hard to hear that message? Why was it important for that person to speak up?
- Read Matthew 3:1–12 aloud.

2 | summarize

Summarize this week's lesson for your child:

Example: *John the Baptist and the prophets of ancient Israel reminded people of God's laws and told them about the coming Savior. They always spoke the truth, bravely and boldly.*

3 | review

Review this week's lesson by asking your child the following questions:

1. Why did God send the prophets? (*The Israelites were worshipping false gods, marrying pagans, and wanting to be like their pagan neighbors. They needed to be reminded of their covenant with God.*)
2. What did the prophets say to the people about their sins? (*They told the people that God would punish them if they didn't repent.*)
3. What did Isaiah say about the Savior? (*He would be born of a virgin and rejected by men.*)
4. What events did Jeremiah foretell? (*Famine, war, and the Babylonian exile.*)
5. What did the people do to Jeremiah? (*They threw him in jail.*)
6. Who was the last and greatest prophet of the Old Testament? (*John the Baptist.*)

References

- Student Textbook: Chapter 10, pp. 46–47
- Sacred Scripture: Is 52:13 — 53:12; Mt 5:3–12
- *Catechism of the Catholic Church:* 62–64, 218, 523, 711–20, 1846–48, 2077

The prophet Isaiah.

4 | apply

Help your child apply this week's lesson by asking the following questions:

1. Have you ever spoken the truth when it was hard? When? What happened?
2. Have you ever been angry with someone who tried to stop you from doing something wrong? Did you listen to that person? Why or why not?
3. If God called you to be a prophet to our world, what might he want you to say?

5 | conclude

- With your child, pray the Our Father.

6 | follow up

During the week, do at least one of the following activities with your child:

1. Memorize 1 Thessalonians 2:4.
2. Read Jeremiah 38. Help your child write and illustrate a story about the events of Jeremiah's life in this chapter.
3. Help your child call a godparent or grandparent and share what he learned about the prophets this week.

> *But just as we have been approved by God to be entrusted with the gospel, so we speak, not to please men, but to please God who tests our hearts.*
> —1 Thessalonians 2:4

notes

_____

_____

_____

_____

_____

_____

_____

Lesson 11

In the Fullness of Time

Lesson Focus | Shortly before the Savior was born, God readied the world for His coming with several miraculous events: the Virgin Mary was conceived and born without Original Sin; in their old age, Elizabeth and Zechariah conceived a child—John the Baptist; and an angel appeared to Mary to tell her that she would be the Savior's Mother. By the power of the Holy Spirit, Mary's visit to Elizabeth was rich in meaning: both Elizabeth and Saint John recognized the Lord; Elizabeth exclaimed that Mary is the Mother of God and prophesied that because of this Mary would be honored; and through Mary's faith God showed his greatness.

1 | begin

- Pray the Glory Be with your child.
- Ask your child what special preparations you would have to make before a very important guest came for dinner. Make suggestions if he needs help.
- Read Matthew 1:18–25 aloud.

2 | summarize

Summarize this week's lesson for your child:

Example: *Just as we would have to make special preparations before an important guest came to our house for dinner, God made very special, even miraculous, preparations before the Savior came into the world.*

3 | review

References

- Student Textbook: Chapter 11, pp. 51–54

- Sacred Scripture: Mt 1:18–25; Lk 1:46–55, 68–79

- *Catechism of the Catholic Church*: 55–58, 148–49, 399–412, 484–95

Review this week's lesson by asking your child the following questions:

1. What happened at the Annunciation? (*The archangel Gabriel told Mary she would be the Mother of God's Son.*)
2. What is the Visitation? (*Mary's visiting her cousin Elizabeth.*)
3. What is the Immaculate Conception? (*Mary's being preserved from sin from the moment she was conceived in her mother's womb.*)
4. What is the Magnificat? (*A hymn of praise sung by Mary at the Visitation.*)
5. Who were John the Baptist's parents? (*Zechariah and Elizabeth.*)
6. What did Zechariah's prophecy foretell? (*The future of John the Baptist.*)
7. Who were Mary's parents? (*Joachim and Anne.*)

4 | apply

Help your child apply this week's lesson by asking the following questions:

1. When an angel told Zechariah that he and his wife would have a child, he didn't believe it. Why do you think he doubted the angel? How should he have reacted? Why?
2. When the angel told Mary what God's plan for her was, she believed and accepted it immediately. How can you follow Mary's example?
3. In the Magnificat, Mary praised God for the miracle he was working in her. For which miracles and blessings should you praise God?

5 | conclude

- With your child, pray the Hail Mary.

6 | follow up

During the week, do at least one of the following activities with your child:

1. Memorize Luke 1:38a.
2. As a family, pray the Magnificat (Lk 1:38–55).
3. Research Saint Bernadette and the apparition of Our Lady of Lourdes.

And Mary said, "Behold, I am the handmaid of the Lord; let it be to me according to your word." And the angel departed from her.
—Luke 1:38

notes

_____
_____
_____
_____
_____
_____
_____
_____

Born in the City of David

Lesson Focus | After Joseph and Mary wed, they traveled to Bethlehem, the city of David, to participate in a census ordered by the emperor. There, in a stable, the Second Person of the Blessed Trinity was born as man. Soon afterward, the Holy Family presented Him at the temple, then fled to Egypt to escape Herod's persecution. After Herod died, they returned to Nazareth.

1 | begin

- Pray the Glory Be with your child.
- Ask your child what he thinks God looks like. After he gives his answer, show him a picture of a tiny baby. Explain that God once looked like that baby.
- Read Luke 2:1–20 aloud.

2 | summarize

Summarize this week's lesson for your child:

Example: *Because God wanted us to be with him forever in heaven, he became one of us. God the Son became a tiny, helpless baby and grew up in a human family much like ours.*

3 | review

Review this week's lesson by asking your child the following questions:

1. How did Joseph know that God wanted him to continue with his plan to marry Mary? (*An angel told him.*)
2. What forced Mary and Joseph to go to Bethlehem? (*The census.*)
3. What did Jewish law require Mary and Joseph to do once Jesus was born? (*Present him in the temple.*)
4. What does *Incarnation* mean? (*God made man; the Son's taking on a human nature.*)

References

- Student Textbook: Chapter 12, pp. 55–58

- Sacred Scripture: Mt 2:1–23; Lk 2:1–20

- *Catechism of the Catholic Church*: 410–12, 456–78, 525–30

Bethlehem.

4 | apply

Help your child apply this week's lesson by asking the following questions:

1. Jesus came into the world as a poor, helpless baby. He made himself one of the littlest creatures in the world out of love for us. How can you be humble like Jesus?
2. God promised Simeon and Anna that they would meet the Savior before they died. They waited many, many years for God to honor that promise. Do you think they ever doubted him? What can you learn from their patience and trust?
3. What does God's willingness to become a man say about his love for us? How can you thank him for that love?

5 | conclude

- With your child, pray the Hail Mary.

6 | follow up

During the week, do at least one of the following activities with your child:

1. Memorize John 3:16.
2. Pick a special family activity to do every day until Christmas to help prepare your hearts for Jesus' coming (e.g., read one Bible story every night, collect change in a jar for a crisis pregnancy center, give up sweets, etc.).
3. Pray the third Joyful Mystery of the Rosary: The Nativity.

For God so loved the world that he gave his only-begotten Son, that whoever believes in him should not perish but have eternal life.
—John 3:16

notes

_____

_____

_____

_____

_____

_____

_____

The Holy Family

Lesson Focus | The Church describes Jesus' childhood as "the hidden years" because little is known about that time. We do know, however, that his family lived in Nazareth, Joseph worked hard as a carpenter, Mary labored long hours caring for her family, and Jesus helped them both. We also know that Jesus was obedient to his parents in every way and that the whole family dedicated themselves to loving God, their neighbors, and one another. In all these ways and more, our families are called to imitate the Holy Family.

1 | begin

- Pray the Glory Be with your child.
- With your child, write out a schedule of your family's typical day. Include details such as cooking, cleaning, prayers, etc. Ask him to look over the list and tell you what your daily family life has in common with the Holy Family's.
- Read Luke 2:41–52 aloud.

2 | summarize

Summarize this week's lesson for your child:

Example: *Even though Jesus was God, his family's life was very ordinary in many ways. They worked hard and loved one another, modeling for us how we're supposed to live as a family.*

3 | review

Review this week's lesson by asking your child the following questions:

1. How many years of Jesus' life are called "the hidden years"? (*Thirty.*)
2. How did Joseph show that he was willing to obey God even in difficult circumstances? (*He first moved his family to Egypt to protect them, then back to Israel when it was safe.*)
3. What was Joseph's job? (*He was a carpenter.*)
4. What work did Mary do? (*She cared for the house and the family—cooking, cleaning, sewing, and more.*)
5. How did the Holy Family show their love for God? (*They prayed and helped the poor.*)
6. How did Jesus show his love for his parents? (*He obeyed them.*)

References

- Student Textbook: Chapter 13, pp. 59–61
- Sacred Scripture: Mt 2:19–23; Lk 2:41–52
- *Catechism of the Catholic Church*: 527–34, 1655–58, 2174–88, 2214–20, 2243–49

4 | apply

Help your child apply this week's lesson by asking the following questions:
1. How is our family like the Holy Family? How are we different?
2. In what ways can you follow the example Jesus set in his family life?
3. How can our family make God more a part of our life? How can we serve him better?

5 | conclude

- With your child, pray the Hail Mary.

6 | follow up

During the week, do at least one of the following activities with your child:
1. Memorize John 15:12.
2. With your child's help, purchase a crucifix for a room in your home where you spend time together as a family (e.g., the living room, TV room, kitchen). After Sunday Mass, ask your priest to bless it for you; then take it home and hang it.
3. Over the weekend, pick one kind act you can do for the poor and do it together as a family. Collect old coats, clothes, or toys and take them to a charity thrift store; donate canned goods to a food pantry, volunteer at a soup kitchen, or take a meal to a family in need.

This is my commandment, that you love one another as I have loved you.
—John 15:12

notes

_____

_____

_____

_____

_____

_____

_____

The Kingdom of Heaven

Lesson Focus | When Jesus was thirty, he began his public ministry with his baptism by Saint John and his preparation in the desert. He then began preaching about the Kingdom of God. Through his sermons and stories, called parables, he taught people that those who wished to enter God's kingdom had to love God and their neighbor, forgive their enemies, seek peace, care for the poor and sick, and do God's will.

1 | begin

- Pray the Glory Be with your child.
- Ask your child to describe some of the characteristics typical of the world's greatest kingdoms (e.g., the Roman Empire). If he needs help, make suggestions: a powerful ruler, a mighty military, great wealth, etc.
- Read Matthew 13:44–46 aloud.

2 | summarize

Summarize this week's lesson for your child:

Example: *Through parables such as those we just read, Jesus taught his followers that the Kingdom of Heaven would be like no earthly kingdom. Helping people understand the Kingdom of Heaven and how to enter it was the central message of Jesus' public ministry.*

References

- Student Textbook: Chapter 14, pp. 62–65

- Sacred Scripture: Mt 3:1–4:25; 13:31–32, 44, 47–51; Mk 4:1–33

- *Catechism of the Catholic Church*: 422–29, 441–45, 456–60, 535–46, 551–53, 2842–45

3 | review

Review this week's lesson by asking your child the following questions:
1. Who was John the Baptist? (*Jesus' cousin and a prophet who preached repentance.*)
2. What did God say at Jesus' baptism? (*"This is my beloved Son in whom I am well pleased."*)
3. For how many days did Jesus pray alone in the desert? (*Forty.*)
4. Why did he go into the desert? (*To pray, fast, and prepare for his public ministry.*)
5. What is the Kingdom of Heaven? (*The Church in heaven, in purgatory, and on earth—all those united with Christ in love.*)
6. Who were the Apostles? (*Twelve men Jesus chose to be his closest followers. They were Simon Peter, Andrew, James the Greater, John, Philip, Bartholomew, Thomas, Matthew, James the Lesser, Jude Thaddeus, Simon, and Judas.*)

4 | apply

Help your child apply this week's lesson by asking the following questions:
1. How can your faith in Jesus, like the mustard seed, change the lives of those you know? What must you do to set a good example for your friends and neighbors?
2. As the treasure in the parable was bought at a great price, we have to make sacrifices to attain the Kingdom of Heaven. What sacrifices have you made for God? What other sacrifices could you make?

5 | conclude

- With your child, pray the Hail Mary.

6 | follow up

During the week, do at least one of the following activities with your child:
1. Memorize Matthew 5:10.
2. Every evening, pray the Prayer to Saint Michael (see Appendix) together asking for help to resist temptation.
3. Research what happened to the twelve Apostles after Jesus' Ascension. Help your child write a story about one of them or dramatize his martyrdom.

Blessed are those who are persecuted for righteousness' sake, for theirs is the kingdom of heaven.
—Matthew 5:10

notes

_____

_____

_____

_____

_____

_____

_____

The Father and I Are One

Lesson Focus | Jesus was the Son of God, truly God and truly man, but he didn't reveal his divinity to others right away. Instead, he first hinted at it through his miracles: he healed the sick, cast out demons, and calmed stormy waters. He then told his Apostles who he was and allowed three of them to see his glory during the Transfiguration. Other signs and statements during his ministry followed, but only a few believed or understood.

1 | begin

- Pray the Glory Be with your child.
- Ask your child how he would react if a friend or neighbor he had known all his life claimed to be God. Would he believe the claim? Why or why not? What would the friend have to do to make you believe him?
- Read Mark 4:35–41 aloud.

2 | summarize

Summarize this week's lesson for your child:

Example: *To show people that he was the Son of God, truly God and truly man, Jesus performed many great miracles. He also allowed a few people to see him in all his glory and to hear his Father's voice. Still, only a few people believed or understood who he was.*

3 | review

Review this week's lesson by asking your child the following questions:

1. How did Peter know that Jesus was God? (*The Father revealed it to him.*)
2. At what event did Jesus unveil his glory to three Apostles? (*The Transfiguration.*)
3. What was the greatest proof of Jesus' divinity? (*The Resurrection.*)
4. What words did Jesus use to claim he was God? (*"I AM."*)
5. When did God the Father speak and testify to Jesus' divinity? (*At Jesus' baptism.*)
6. By what power did Jesus perform miracles? (*His own divine power.*)

References

- Student Textbook: Chapter 15, pp. 66–69
- Sacred Scripture: Mt 14:22–33; 16:13–20; 17:1–8; Mk 1:21–45; 4:35–41; 5:1–20; Jn 9:35–38
- *Catechism of the Catholic Church*: 441–45, 464–70, 547–56, 1503–5, 2148

4 | apply

Help your child apply this week's lesson by asking the following questions:

1. Why do you think Jesus didn't reveal who he was right away? Why was this wise?
2. Jesus showed people the truth about who he was by his actions first. What actions can you perform to help people know that you love and believe in Christ?
3. If someone asked you why you believe that Jesus is the Son of God, what would you say?

5 | conclude

- With your child, pray the Hail Mary.

6 | follow up

During the week, do at least one of the following activities with your child:

1. Memorize John 10:30.
2. As a family, pray the fourth Luminous Mystery of the Rosary: The Transfiguration of our Lord. Begin by reading aloud the account in Matthew 17:1–8.
3. Research Saint Martin de Porres, the first black saint of the Americas, and the many miracles he performed by God's power.

I and the Father are one.
—John 10:30

notes

_____

_____

_____

_____

_____

_____

_____

Lesson 16

Your Sins Are Forgiven

Lesson Focus | To help the Jews understand that he was God, Jesus forgave people's sins. Although we all can forgive someone who sins against us, we don't have the authority to forgive someone whose sin doesn't hurt us. But God has the authority to forgive all sins because all sin is an offense against him. Through his actions, Jesus taught us that God wants to forgive our sins and that there is no sin too great for him to forgive. As long as we repent and ask for forgiveness, God will be merciful. In return, he asks that we respond in the same way to those who hurt us.

1 | begin

- Pray the Glory Be with your child.
- Remind your child of a time he disobeyed you and tried to hide what he did from you. Ask him why he hid his disobedience. Did he think you wouldn't forgive him?
- Read Luke 15:1–10 aloud.

2 | summarize

Summarize this week's lesson for your child:

Example: *In those parables, Jesus is talking about himself. Just like any good parent, God always forgives us when we repent of our sins. In fact, he rejoices when we say we're sorry. He wants to forgive us, and there is no sin too big for him to forgive.*

3 | review

Review this week's lesson by asking your child the following questions:

1. How did Jesus show that he is the Son of God? (*By performing miracles — healing, casting out devils, calming the wind and waters, calling people from death — and by forgiving sins.*)
2. Who can forgive sins? (*Only God can forgive sins.*)
3. What is needed to receive God's forgiveness? (*To repent and to ask.*)
4. Name three people in the Gospels who converted. (*Mary Magdalene, Zacchaeus, the good thief, etc.*)

References

- Student Textbook: Chapter 16, pp. 70–72

- Sacred Scripture: Mt 6:9–15; 18:23–35; Mk 2; Lk 15; 19:1–10; 23:39–43

- *Catechism of the Catholic Church*: 468–69, 574–82, 1441–42, 1829, 1846–48, 2842–45

4 | apply

Help your child apply this week's lesson by asking the following questions:
1. From whom have you had to ask for forgiveness? Did the person forgive you? How did that make you feel?
2. Who has asked for your forgiveness? Did you forgive that person? Was it hard? Why?
3. How can we show God that we truly forgive someone? Why should we forgive others?

5 | conclude

- With your child, pray the Hail Mary.

6 | follow up

During the week, do at least one of the following activities with your child:
1. Memorize Matthew 6:14.
2. Have your child review the examination of conscience in the Appendix. Then, as a family, go to confession.
3. Practice verbalizing forgiveness. When your child disobeys and apologizes, tell him, "I forgive you." When a sibling or friend apologizes to him, ask him always to respond, "I forgive you."

For if you forgive men their trespasses, your heavenly Father also will forgive you.
—Matthew 6:14

notes

_____
_____
_____
_____
_____
_____
_____

Lesson 17

True God and True Man

Lesson Focus | Although Jesus was really and truly God, he was also really and truly human. Like all men, he felt hunger, tiredness, pleasure, pain, fear, and joy. Although as God he existed from all eternity, at a certain point in time, he took on a human nature and was born of the Virgin Mary. As a man, he didn't just tell us how to live, love, and obey God. He actually showed us, becoming our model in all things.

1 | begin

- Pray the Glory Be with your child.
- Search online for images of Jesus (or look at several you may have in your home). Ask your child which image he likes best and why. What type of person does Jesus look like?
- Read Matthew 19:13–15 aloud.

2 | summarize

Summarize this week's lesson for your child:

Example: *Although Jesus was God, he was also man. He felt much that we feel and did much that we do. He loved children, got tired, and felt both happy and sad. As a man, he taught us how to live. He set for each of us the perfect example of love and obedience.*

References

- Student Textbook: Chapter 17, pp. 73–75

- Sacred Scripture: Mt 14:19; 25:40; Mk 1:22; Lk 6:29; 10:27; 23:34; Jn 13:34; 14:15

- *Catechism of the Catholic Church*: 456–78, 2607–16, 2842–45

3 | review

Review this week's lesson by asking your child the following questions:

1. What is a person? (*Who someone is; an intelligent being with intellect and will.*)
2. What is a nature? (*What a thing is; the essence of a thing.*)
3. What is the hypostatic union? (*The union of a divine nature and human nature in the one Divine Person Jesus Christ.*)
4. As the Second Person of the Blessed Trinity, Jesus is _____. (*God.*)
5. As a man, Jesus is our _____. (*Brother and friend.*)
6. What do we call the event in which Jesus became man? (*The Incarnation.*)

Jesus accepts his Father's will in the Garden of Gethsemane.

4 | apply

Help your child apply this week's lesson by asking the following questions:

1. How did Jesus teach us to obey God? How can you be more obedient like Jesus?
2. What else did Jesus teach us to do? How well do you do those things? How could you do better?
3. When you're unsure of what is the right thing to do, how can Jesus help you?

5 | conclude

- With your child, pray the Hail Mary.

6 | follow up

During the week, do at least one of the following activities with your child:

1. Memorize John 1:14.
2. Print out or purchase a copy of the image of Jesus your child liked best from Step 1 of this lesson. Frame it and hang it in his room or pin it to a bulletin board near his desk.
3. Help your child pick three to five things Jesus felt and did that your child feels and does (e.g., eating, crying, sleeping, studying, etc.). Have him draw pictures of himself and Jesus doing those things, side by side.

And the Word became flesh and dwelt among us, full of grace and truth; we have beheld his glory, glory as of the only-begotten Son from the Father.
—John 1:14

notes

_____

_____

_____

_____

_____

_____

_____

_____

Rejected by the Proud

Lesson Focus | Jesus was a very different Savior from the one many Jews were expecting. He wasn't rich or powerful. He wasn't interested in leading an earthly kingdom. And he rejected the company of the religious leaders (especially the scribes, Pharisees, and Sadducees), preferring the company of sinners and the poor. He also made people uncomfortable with his teachings on sin, the Eucharist, and forgiveness. For this, both then and now, many people have rejected Him.

1 | begin

- Pray the Glory Be with your child.
- Ask your child about a time he did something wrong and was corrected by a friend, a teacher, or a neighbor. How did that make him feel? Embarrassed? Ashamed? Angry?
- Read Matthew 23:1–12 aloud.

2 | summarize

Summarize this week's lesson for your child:

Example: *The Pharisees, Sadducees, and other Jewish leaders didn't like it when Jesus corrected them, nor did they approve of his popularity with the poor. Rather than repent and change their ways, they rejected him and looked for ways to silence him.*

3 | review

Review this week's lesson by asking your child the following questions:

1. How were Jesus' teachings on the Eucharist received? (*People didn't like what he said and stopped following him.*)
2. Who were the important Jews at the time of Jesus? (*There were a number of groups, including the Pharisees, the Sadducees, and scribes.*)
3. Why did some people think that Jesus was not the Messiah? (*They expected the Messiah to have great earthly power and status, and to follow the Law in the way they did.*)
4. How do we reject Jesus? (*Through sin.*)

References

- Student Textbook: Chapter 18, pp. 76–78

- Sacred Scripture: Is 52:13–53:12; Mt 14:15–21; Jn 2:1–11; 5:36; 6:35–39; 14:15; Acts 1:6–7

- *Catechism of the Catholic Church*: 574–94, 1849–66, 1961–64, 2142–45

4 | apply

Help your child apply this week's lesson by asking the following questions:

1. What are some things you've done that have been a rejection of Jesus?
2. What are some things you've done that have shown you accept Jesus as your Savior?
3. What can you do for God to help make up for all the things people do to reject Him?

5 | conclude

- With your child, pray the Hail Mary.

6 | follow up

During the week, do at least one of the following activities with your child:

1. Memorize 1 Peter 5:5b.
2. Pray for fifteen minutes in your parish's Adoration Chapel or in front of your church's tabernacle.
3. On Friday, in addition to abstaining from meat, help your child pick one thing he can do to let Jesus know he loves him and to make up for others' rejection of him. This could include a visit to an elderly neighbor, saying a prayer for someone in need, doing something kind for a classmate, reading a Bible story, or performing another kind or prayerful act.

Clothe yourselves, all of you, with humility toward one another, for "God opposes the proud, but gives grace to the humble."
—1 Peter 5:5

notes

_____

_____

_____

_____

_____

_____

_____

The Acceptance of the Father's Will

Lesson Focus | Just as Mary yielded her will to God's at the Incarnation, so Christ yielded his will in the events leading up to his Passion and death. His entrance into Jerusalem, the Last Supper and the institution of the Eucharist, the scourging he received, and his death on the Cross were all willingly accepted by him because he knew they were all a necessary part of God's plan of salvation.

1 | begin

- Pray the Glory Be with your child.
- Tell your child about a time you freely chose to do something very difficult (e.g., walked away from a bad friendship, spoke against injustice, left your job, etc.). Explain how you struggled before making the choice and why you made the choice you did.
- Read John 10:11–18 aloud.

2 | summarize

Summarize this week's lesson for your child:

Example: *Jesus was God. If he had wanted to stop the Roman and Jewish leaders, he could have. But he didn't. He chose to suffer and die because it was part of God's plan to save us.*

References

- Student Textbook: Chapter 19, pp. 79–82

- Sacred Scripture: Mt 26:30–56; Mk 15:1–26; Lk 18:31–33; 22:14–20; Jn 11:1–53; 13; 19:18–30

- *Catechism of the Catholic Church*: 599–618, 963–70, 1333–44, 1371–81, 2598–2606

3 | review

Review this week's lesson by asking your child the following questions:

1. The week before his death, what feast did Jesus go to Jerusalem to celebrate? (*Passover.*)
2. What did Jesus tell his Apostles about his future? (*That he would die on the Cross and rise from the dead on the third day.*)
3. What two Sacraments did Jesus institute at the Last Supper? (*The Eucharist and Holy Orders.*)
4. What did Jesus say to the Father in the Garden of Gethsemane? (*"Thy will be done."*)
5. From the Cross, whom did Jesus give us to be our Mother? (*Mary.*)
6. Name the Sorrowful Mysteries of the Rosary in order. (*The Agony in the Garden, the Scourging at the Pillar, the Crowning with Thorns, the Carrying of the Cross, the Crucifixion.*)

4 | apply

Help your child apply this week's lesson by asking the following questions:

1. Have you ever done something difficult because it was the right thing to do? When? Why? How did you make your decision?
2. What does the choice Jesus made to suffer and die say about his love for you?
3. How can you follow Jesus' example of obedience and sacrifice every day?

5 | conclude

- With your child, pray the Hail Holy Queen (see Appendix).

6 | follow up

During the week, do at least one of the following activities with your child:

1. Memorize Matthew 26:39.
2. On Friday, visit your parish to pray the Stations of the Cross (see Appendix).
3. Pick a day on which everyone in the family will work at not complaining about any of the trials or tasks they face that day. Give a small reward — such as ice cream or chocolate — to everyone who succeeds.

And going a little farther he fell on his face and prayed, "My Father, if it be possible, let this chalice pass from me; nevertheless, not as I will, but as you will."
—Matthew 26:39

notes

_____

_____

_____

_____

_____

_____

_____

Lesson 20

The Perfect Sacrifice

Lesson Focus | Since his beginning, man has always offered sacrifices to God in order to atone for his sins. No sacrifice, however, could truly atone for sin because no sacrifice was perfect. Jesus' offering of himself on the Cross, however, was. That's because Jesus, who both offered the sacrifice and was the sacrifice, was perfect. At every Mass, Jesus, through the priest, continues to offer himself to God when the bread and wine are transformed into his Body and Blood. It is the same sacrifice offered on Calvary, re–presented in time.

1 | begin

- Pray the Glory Be with your child.
- Show your child pictures of sheep, goats, calves, doves, wheat, and wine. Explain that if you had lived in Jerusalem during Jesus' time, your family would have gone to the temple to give these items to the priest for sacrifice.
- Together read John 1:19–30 aloud.

2 | summarize

Summarize this week's lesson for your child:

Example: *When Jesus offered his life on the Cross, he became the one, perfect sacrifice, the Lamb of God offered up for all the world's sins. After that, it was no longer necessary for people to offer up other ritual sacrifices, such as goats, lambs, and doves.*

3 | review

Review this week's lesson by asking your child the following questions:

1. What is a sacrifice? (*The offering up of something to God.*)
2. What does it mean to redeem something? (*To buy it back, to pay the price for it.*)
3. What is a religious persecution? (*Attacking a person for practicing the Faith.*)
4. What is a martyr? (*A person who is killed for practicing the Faith.*)
5. What was accomplished by Christ's sacrifice on the Cross that was not accomplished by the Old Testament sacrifices? (*It redeemed man from sin, opened the gates of heaven, and was a sacrifice offered for everyone.*)
6. How do we receive the grace of Christ's sacrifice on the Cross? (*By participating in the Mass, which is the same sacrifice re-presented in time.*)

References

- Student Textbook: Chapter 20, pp. 83–86
- Sacred Scripture: Mk 12:41–44; Jn 1:29
- *Catechism of the Catholic Church*: 464–78, 1023–37, 1356–81, 2099–2100, 2473–74

4 | apply

Help your child apply this week's lesson by asking the following questions:

1. When you go to Mass, how can you show Christ that you understand he's offering himself for you in the Holy Eucharist and that you are grateful for his sacrifice?
2. When you make little sacrifices out of love for Christ, what should your attitude be?
3. Has anyone ever teased you because of your Catholic Faith? What happened? What did you do? If it never has happened, what do you think you would do if it did?

5 | conclude

- With your child, pray the Hail Mary.

6 | follow up

During the week, do at least one of the following activities with your child:

1. Memorize Ephesians 5:2.
2. As a family, attend a weekday or Saturday morning Mass in addition to Sunday Mass.
3. Learn more about Saint Edmund Campion and the English martyrs.

> *And walk in love, as Christ loved us and gave himself up for us, a fragrant offering and sacrifice to God.*
> *—Ephesians 5:2*

notes

_____

_____

_____

_____

_____

_____

_____

Lesson 21

He Is Risen

Lesson Focus | On the Sunday morning after Jesus died, Mary Magdalene and some other women went to his tomb. They found the large stone rolled away and his body gone. Soon after this, Jesus himself appeared, first to Mary Magdalene and later to the disciples. As he had foretold, he had risen from the dead. He wasn't a ghost. He still had a body that could eat and that people could touch. But it was a resurrected body, different, transformed. By rising from the dead, Christ made it possible for all who believe in him also to rise from the dead.

1 | begin

- Pray the Glory Be with your child.
- Ask your child what his favorite thing about Easter is.
- Read Matthew 28:1–9 aloud.

2 | summarize

Summarize this week's lesson for your child:

Example: *We have so much fun on Easter because we celebrate what happened on the first Easter morning long ago—Jesus' Resurrection from the dead. We also celebrate what all who love and follow Jesus will receive when they die—eternal life with him.*

3 | review

Review this week's lesson by asking your child the following questions:

1. Why did the women go to the tomb on Easter? (*To complete the Jewish burial customs and anoint Jesus' body.*)
2. How did they know he was resurrected? (*Although guards were there, the stone was rolled away and the body gone. An angel told them he had been raised, and later many people saw Jesus himself.*)
3. What does the Resurrection tell us about Jesus? (*He is God.*)
4. What does the Resurrection tell us about those who follow Jesus? (*If we die in friendship with him, we too will be raised from the dead and live forever in heaven.*)
5. When do we celebrate Jesus' Resurrection? (*On Easter and every Sunday.*)

References

- Student Textbook: Chapter 21, pp. 87–90

- Sacred Scripture: Mt 27:55—28:8; Mk 16:1–5, 14; Lk 23:53—24:49; Jn 20:1–28; 21:5–14

- *Catechism of the Catholic Church*: 631–58

4 | apply

Help your child apply this week's lesson by asking the following questions:

1. This year, how can we make our celebration of Easter extra special and show Jesus that we know that remembering his Resurrection is the most important thing about the day?
2. What can our family do every Sunday to celebrate Jesus' Resurrection in a special way?
3. Why should you be grateful for the gift of your body? How can you show God you're grateful for that gift?

5 | conclude

- With your child, pray the Hail Mary.

6 | follow up

During the week, do at least one of the following activities with your child:

1. Memorize 1 Corinthians 6:19–20.
2. Pray the first Glorious Mystery of the Rosary: The Resurrection.
3. Find or take pictures of your child doing his favorite activities (e.g., reading, playing soccer, cooking, laughing, etc.). Put together a collage of those pictures and write at the top or bottom: "I thank God for my body because I can..."

Do you not know that your body is a temple of the Holy Spirit within you, which you have from God? You are not your own.
—1 Corinthians 6:19–20

notes

_____

_____

_____

_____

_____

_____

_____

Jesus Sends the Apostles

Lesson Focus | After his Resurrection, Jesus appeared to the Apostles many times, giving them the authority to forgive sins, teaching them all they needed to know to build his Church, and commissioning them to baptize people in his name. Before his Ascension, he made Peter the first leader of the Church—the Pope. Today, Jesus remains present in both the Church and the world. He asks us to love him by loving the Church and our neighbors.

1 | begin

- Pray the Glory Be with your child.
- Show your child a picture of the Vatican and Saint Peter's Basilica in Rome. Remind him that the Pope, Peter's successor, lives there, and that Saint Peter's is the visible sign of the Church that Christ established on earth, the Church to which we belong.
- Read Matthew 28:18–20 aloud.

2 | summarize

Summarize this week's lesson for your child:

Example: *Jesus told his disciples to build his Church—a worldwide family of people who love and follow Jesus. During the forty days between his Resurrection and Ascension, Jesus prepared his Apostles in a special way for that work.*

References

- Student Textbook: Chapter 22, pp. 91–94

- Sacred Scripture: Mt 25:31–46; 28:19; Lk 24:13–35; Jn 20:21–23; 21; Acts 1:1–14

- *Catechism of the Catholic Church*: 659–64, 782–86, 858–62, 880–913, 2443–49, 2012–16

3 | review

Review this week's lesson by asking your child the following questions:

1. How long did Jesus spend with his disciples after his Resurrection? (*Forty days.*)
2. What did Jesus do with his disciples before his Ascencion? (*Strengthened their faith, helped them understand his teachings, and instructed them on how to spread the gospel.*)
3. What power did Jesus give to his disciples after his Resurrection? (*The power to forgive sins.*)
4. Before his Ascension, whom did Jesus name as the visible head of his Church? (*Peter.*)

4 | apply

Help your child apply this week's lesson by asking the following questions:

1. How does the Church help you know and love Jesus? How can you show Jesus that you're grateful for the gift of his Church?
2. What does it mean to see Jesus in others? When is it difficult to see Jesus in others? How should we act toward other people?

5 | conclude

- With your child, pray the Hail Mary.

6 | follow up

During the week, do at least one of the following activities with your child:

1. Memorize Matthew 16:18.
2. Invite a single, widowed, or divorced person to join your family for Sunday dinner. Let your child help with the meal planning and preparations.
3. Make a list of people you know who are in need of prayers. Write out their names on a chalkboard or white board, and include them in your prayers at night.

And I tell you, you are Peter, and on this rock I will build my Church, and the gates of Hades shall not prevail against it.
—Matthew 16:18

notes

_____

_____

_____

_____

_____

_____

_____

The Giver of Life

Lesson Focus | Ten days after Jesus' Ascension, the Holy Spirit came into the Apostles' hearts, giving them the strength and courage to preach the gospel fearlessly. The Holy Spirit is the Third Person of the Blessed Trinity. He shares the same nature as the Father and the Son, and his mission in the world is to guide and lead the Church, ensuring that the Pope and the bishops teach the truth about Jesus and helping Christians to live good, holy lives.

1 | begin

- Pray the Glory Be with your child.
- Show your child pictures of a dove and a flame. Ask him why he thinks those symbols are used to represent the Holy Spirit. Of what do the two things remind him?
- Read Acts 2:1–21 aloud.

2 | summarize

Summarize this week's lesson for your child:

Example: *The Holy Spirit is the Third Person of the Blessed Trinity. He is our comforter and our teacher. He brings peace, like the dove. He also makes us strong, courageous, and bold, giving us the passion, or fire, to proclaim and live the gospel.*

3 | review

Review this week's lesson by asking your child the following questions:

1. Is the Holy Spirit God? (*Yes.*)
2. For how many days after the Ascension did the Apostles wait for the Holy Spirit? (*Nine.*)
3. What happened immediately after the Holy Spirit descended? (*The Apostles could speak in many languages, Peter proclaimed the gospel, and over three thousand people were baptized.*)
4. How does the Holy Spirit help guide the Church? (*He protects the Pope and all the bishops in union with the Pope from teaching error in matters of faith and morals.*)
5. When does the Holy Spirit first come to us? (*At Baptism.*)

References

- Student Textbook: Chapter 23, pp. 97–100
- Sacred Scripture: Gen 1:1–2; Is 11:2; Mt 3:16; Lk 1:35; Jn 15:26; 20:22; Acts 2
- *Catechism of the Catholic Church*: 238–56, 683–90, 702–41, 1266, 1303

4 | apply

Help your child apply this week's lesson by asking the following questions:

1. Which of the Holy Spirit's gifts could help you with a problem you're facing right now? How? What do you think you could do to receive more of that gift?
2. Is the Holy Spirit in you? How might people see that the Holy Spirit is in you?

5 | conclude

- With your child, pray the Come, Holy Spirit prayer (see Appendix).

6 | follow up

During the week, do at least one of the following activities with your child:

1. Memorize Romans 14:17.
2. Ask your child to write out the Come, Holy Spirit prayer (see Appendix), and work on memorizing it by praying it together as a family.
3. Plan a party for Pentecost. Incorporate into the decorations symbols of the Holy Spirit, as well as the color red—the liturgical color for the feast.

> *For the kingdom of God does not mean food and drink but righteousness and peace and joy in the Holy Spirit.*
> —Romans 14:17

notes

_____

_____

_____

_____

_____

_____

_____

Lesson 24

The Mystical Body

Lesson Focus | Both before and after His Resurrection, Jesus prepared his Apostles to build and lead his Church on earth. He also left Peter in charge as the first Pope. The Church is more than an organization: it is the Mystical Body of Christ. All who belong to the Church—in heaven, in purgatory, and on earth—are part of Christ's Body. Christ is the head and the Holy Spirit the soul. Those who love Jesus but are not Catholic are separated members of the Body, and we're called to pray that they will be reunited with us in faith.

1 | begin

- Pray the Glory Be with your child.
- Ask your child to describe what the different parts of his body help him to do. How do those parts help each other? When one part is hurting, how does this affect the others?
- Read 1 Corinthians 12:13–21, 26–27 aloud.

2 | summarize

Summarize this week's lesson for your child:

Example: *The Church isn't just an organization. It's a Mystical Body—the Body of Christ. Because of your Baptism, you are a part of that Body, united to every other person, living or dead, who loves Christ and believes in the teachings of the Catholic Church.*

References

- Student Textbook: Chapter 24, pp. 101–103
- Sacred Scripture: Mt 16:13–20; Jn 17; 1 Cor 12:13–21
- *Catechism of the Catholic Church*: 758–69, 782–96, 861–62, 880–913, 946–59, 1030–32

3 | review

Review this week's lesson by asking your child the following questions:

1. Who founded the Church and is the head of the Mystical Body? (*Jesus Christ.*)
2. Who is the visible head of the Mystical Body on earth? (*The Pope.*)
3. What is the Communion of Saints? (*All the faithful, in heaven, in purgatory, and on earth, united in Christ.*)
4. How can we help the souls in purgatory to enter heaven? (*By our prayers and sacrifices.*)
5. Why did Christ establish the Church? (*To continue his work on earth and to give his followers both the means to attain holiness and salvation and a secure guide as we strive to achieve them.*)

4 | apply

Help your child apply this week's lesson by asking the following questions:

1. What are some of the different jobs people have in the Body of Christ? When people do those jobs well, how does that help you to know and love Christ better? If people didn't do them well, how could that be harmful?
2. What are some of the other ways in which members of the Body of Christ can help each other?
3. What is your job right now in the Body of Christ? How well are you doing that job? How can you do it better?

5 | conclude

- With your child, pray the Come, Holy Spirit prayer (see Appendix).

6 | follow up

During the week, do at least one of the following activities with your child:

1. Memorize 1 Corinthians 12:27.
2. At your church, light a candle and say a prayer for deceased friends and relatives.
3. Research different Catholic relief organizations and missionary endeavors (ask your priest or Catholic friends for suggestions if necessary) and pick one that your family can begin supporting monthly. Display photos of the people you help, and as a family, read updates from the organization when you receive them.

Now you are the body of Christ and individually members of it.
—1 Corinthians 12:27

notes

_____

_____

_____

_____

_____

_____

_____

Lesson 25

The Identity of the Church

Lesson Focus | In the first few centuries of Christianity, the Church Fathers established four signs, or "marks," by which people could identify the one, true Church of Christ. We repeat these marks every time we say the Nicene Creed during Mass. The Church is *one*, *holy*, *catholic*, and *apostolic*. Of all the religions and Christian communities in the world, the Catholic Church alone possesses all four of those signs.

1 | begin

- Pray the Glory Be with your child.
- Ask your child to pretend to give someone directions to your house. How would he explain how to tell your house apart from other houses?
- Read John 10:2–16 aloud.

2 | summarize

Summarize this week's lesson for your child:

Example: *Christ knows those who belong to him and wants those who follow him to know his Church. We know the Church by the four marks: she is one, holy, catholic, and apostolic.*

3 | review

References

- Student Textbook: Chapter 25, pp. 104–106

- Sacred Scripture: Mt 9:36; 18:12; Mk 14:27; Jn 3:29; 15:1–5; 2 Cor 11:2; Rev 19:7; 21:2, 9

- *Catechism of the Catholic Church*: 77–79, 751–69, 787–96, 811–65, 2683–84

Review this week's lesson by asking your child the following questions:

1. How is the Catholic Church "one"? (*She is one because all her members profess the same faith and share in the same Sacraments. There aren't different versions of the Catholic Faith. The source of that unity is the Blessed Trinity, and the Church's founder is Christ.*)
2. How is the Church "holy"? (*Although her individual members sin, the Church is holy because Christ, her invisible head, gave his life for her and sent the Holy Spirit to give her life and to make her members holy, especially through the Sacraments.*)
3. How is the Church "catholic"? (*Catholic means universal. The Church was instituted for all men and extends to every part of the world.*)
4. How is the Church "apostolic"? (*She was founded upon the Apostles and their preaching and is governed by an unbroken line of their successors—the bishops—who have transmitted the teaching of Christ and the Apostles without change or error.*)
5. Name a few symbols of the Church. (*Sheepfold, vineyard, ship/bark.*)

4 | apply

Help your child apply this week's lesson by asking the following questions:
1. In what ways is the Church like a sheepfold?
2. In what ways is the Church like a ship?
3. In what ways is the Church like a mother?

5 | conclude

- With your child, pray the Come, Holy Spirit prayer (see Appendix).

6 | follow up

During the week, do at least one of the following activities with your child:
1. Memorize 1 Corinthians 14:12.
2. Look up the Pope's intentions for the month. Include them in bedtime prayers.
3. Learn about Saint Isaac Jogues and his companions. Illustrate or dramatize the events leading up to their martyrdom.

> *So with yourselves; since you are eager for manifestations of the Spirit, strive to excel in building up the Church.*
> —1 Corinthians 14:12

notes

_____

_____

_____

_____

_____

_____

_____

The Church Rules

Lesson Focus | Although the Church herself is holy, her members are flawed human beings, working on becoming holy, but not perfectly holy yet. Accordingly, our understanding of Christ's teachings and our ability to live them is often flawed. To make sure that his teachings were properly understood and passed on, Christ gave to his Apostles the power to interpret Scripture and Tradition and make decisions based on those interpretations. That power has been handed down over the years through the Church's bishops.

1 | begin

- Pray the Glory Be with your child.
- Show your child a picture of the Pope. Ask if he knows who it is. If you've ever met or seen the Pope or been to the Vatican, tell your child about that occasion.
- Read John 21:15–17 aloud.

2 | summarize

Summarize this week's lesson for your child:

Example: *Jesus called Peter to be the first Pope, the first leader of his Church on earth. Peter's successors, along with the Apostles' successors, the bishops, have guided the Church ever since, teaching the truth about Christ and helping Catholics to know and do what's right.*

References

- Student Textbook: Chapter 26, pp. 107–9

- Sacred Scripture: Mt 16:16–19; Jn 21:15–17; Acts 6:1–6; 10:1–48; 15:7

- *Catechism of the Catholic Church*: 758–69, 861–62, 871–96, 1554–71, 2041–43

3 | review

Review this week's lesson by asking your child the following questions:

1. How can the Church be both human and divine? (*Her members are human, and her founder, Jesus, is divine.*)
2. Who settled disagreements about the Faith in the early Church? (*The Apostles.*)
3. What are the three degrees of Holy Orders? (*Deacon, priest, and bishop.*)
4. Who is the minister of the Sacrament of Holy Orders? (*The bishop.*)
5. What is a precept of the Church? Name the Church's five precepts. (*Something that every Catholic must do; 1. Attend Mass every Sunday and Holy Day of Obligation; 2. Fast and abstain on appointed days; 3. Go to confession at least once a year; 4. Receive Holy Communion during the Easter season; 5. Contribute to the support of the Church.*)

4 | apply

Help your child apply this week's lesson by asking the following questions:

1. The Pope, bishops, and priests have a very important job to do for the Church. How do you think you can help them do their job?
2. What do you think the Church would be like if we had no Pope or bishops to guard Christ's teachings and settle disputes about what's true?
3. How well does our family observe the precepts of the Church? How can we do a better job?

5 | conclude

- With your child, pray the Come Holy, Spirit prayer (see Appendix).

6 | follow up

During the week, do at least one of the following activities with your child:

1. Memorize Hebrews 13:17a.
2. During evening or morning prayers, pray for your bishop, priest(s), and deacon(s).
3. Visit your diocesan cathedral. Explain to your child that it is the church of your bishop.

> *Obey your leaders and submit to them; for they are keeping watch over your souls, as men who will have to give account.*
> *—Hebrews 13:17*

notes

_____

_____

_____

_____

_____

_____

_____

Teach All Nations

Lesson Focus | To ensure that the Faith is handed on without error, the Holy Spirit gives the Pope the gift of infallibility, which means that when he teaches about faith or morals, his teaching will have no errors. The same gift is given to the bishops when they hold an ecumenical council and are in union with the Pope. The Church has an obligation to safeguard and to spread Christ's teachings. By virtue of our Baptism, we share in that obligation and are bound to evangelize all people through our words and witness.

1 | begin

- Pray the Glory Be with your child.
- Show your child your family Bible. Ask him how this book is different from other books. How do we know it's different?
- Read 2 Thessalonians 2:15 aloud.

2 | summarize

Summarize this week's lesson for your child:

Example: *Without the Holy Bible, there's so much we wouldn't know about God or Jesus. But without the Church, we wouldn't have the Bible. With the help of the Holy Spirit, she has preserved and safeguarded the truth about God's Word and taught that truth to all nations.*

3 | review

Review this week's lesson by asking your child the following questions:
1. What is Sacred Scripture? (*The written Word of God.*)
2. What is Sacred Tradition? (*Everything handed on to us from the Apostles.*)
3. What is infallibility? (*Freedom from error in the teachings of the universal Church in matters of faith and morals.*)
4. What is the magisterium? (*The teaching body of the Church — the Pope and bishops in union with him.*)
5. What is evangelization? (*Spreading the gospel message.*)
6. What is an ecumenical council? (*A gathering of bishops from around the world to make decisions about how to teach and govern the Church.*)

References

- Student Textbook: Chapter 27, pp. 110–12

- Sacred Scripture: Luke 5:1; Jn 21:24–25; 2 Thess 2:15

- *Catechism of the Catholic Church*: 75–79, 105–8, 731–41, 758–69, 849–56, 861–62, 871–96

4 | apply

Help your child apply this week's lesson by asking the following questions:
1. How can you be an evangelist every day through your actions?
2. How can you be an evangelist through your words?
3. Why do you think it's important to teach others about Christ and the Gospel?

5 | conclude

- With your child, pray the Come, Holy Spirit prayer (see Appendix).

6 | follow up

During the week, do at least one of the following activities with your child:
1. Memorize 2 Thessalonians 2:15.
2. Learn more about the work done today by missionaries, such as FOCUS, the Dominicans' East Africa Mission, Catholic Relief Services, or Catholic Medical Missions Board. Pick one group to pray for every day.
3. Have your child call a grandparent, godparent, or family friend and tell about what he learned this week in religion class.

So then, brethren, stand firm and hold to the traditions which you were taught by us, either by word of mouth or by letter.
—2 Thessalonians 2:15

notes

_____
_____
_____
_____
_____
_____
_____

Lesson 28

Called to Holiness

Lesson Focus | God calls all his children to holiness. He wants each of us to become the most perfect image of him we can be and to be fully the person he made us to be. Christ died on the Cross so that we might become holy, and through the Sacraments, he gives us the grace he won for us. Our job as Catholics is to receive that grace and strive to overcome our tendency to sin. We are also called to help others know Christ and to become holy.

1 | begin

- Pray the Glory Be with your child.
- Show your child pictures taken on the day he was baptized, the day he made his first confession, and the day he received his First Communion.
- Read Matthew 5:43–48 aloud.

2 | summarize

Summarize this week's lesson for your child:

Example: *Christ wants us to be more than just nice or good people; he wants us to be saints, perfectly the people he made us to be. The Sacraments help us become saints. They give us the grace Christ won for us. Our job is to receive the Sacraments and overcome sin.*

References

- Student Textbook: Chapter 28, pp. 113–18
- Sacred Scripture: Mt 19:4–12; Jn 16:7–15; 20:21–23; 1 Cor 11:23–26; Eph 5:28–32; Jas 5:14–15
- *Catechism of the Catholic Church*: 55–58, 1117–34, 1145–62, 1425–84, 1846–64

3 | review

Review this week's lesson by asking your child the following questions:

1. What is the difference between Original Sin and actual sin? (*Original Sin is inherited from Adam and Eve. It gives us the tendency to commit sin. Actual sins are sins we commit.*)
2. What is the difference between mortal sin and venial sins? (*Mortal sins are serious sins that we know are serious sins and freely commit. Venial sins are lesser sins or they are serious sins we commit without complete freedom or without full knowledge of their seriousness.*)
3. Do we have to go to confession when we commit venial sins? (*We have to go to confession only when we commit mortal sins, but we should confess venial sins as well.*)
4. What are the seven Sacraments? (*Baptism, Penance, Eucharist, Confirmation, Holy Orders, Marriage, Anointing of the Sick.*)
5. Should you receive Holy Communion in a state of mortal sin? (*No, that too is a mortal sin.*)
6. What do the Sacraments do for us? (*They help us receive God's grace, avoid sin, and grow in holiness.*)

4 | apply

Help your child apply this week's lesson by asking the following questions:

1. How is your relationship with God like your relationship with your parents?
2. How does God show His love for you?
3. How can you show your love for God?

5 | conclude

- With your child, pray the Come, Holy Spirit prayer (see Appendix).

6 | follow up

During the week, do at least one of the following activities with your child:

1. Memorize Matthew 5:48.
2. As a family, go to confession on Saturday or during the week.
3. Research your child's patron saint, and find out why he was considered holy. Who is he known for helping?

> *You, therefore, must be perfect, as your heavenly Father is perfect.*
> —Matthew 5:48

notes

_____

_____

_____

_____

_____

_____

_____

The Mother of God in Our Lives

Lesson Focus | Just as Eve, the mother of the human race, helped bring sin and death into the world when she disobeyed God, Mary brought life and grace through her obedience. This is one of the reasons she is called the New Eve, the new Mother of humanity. From the Cross, Christ declared Mary the Mother of all who are his disciples. She intercedes for us with her Son and offers us help and guidance. She also gave us the Rosary, a prayer that helps us meditate upon the mysteries of Christ's life and hers.

1 | begin

- Pray the Glory Be with your child.
- Ask your child what a mother's job is. How does she care for her children? What does she teach them? Provide for them? Ask of them?
- Read John 19:26–27 aloud.

2 | summarize

Summarize this week's lesson for your child:

Example: *From the Cross, Jesus gave us his Mother, Mary, to be our own Mother in faith. Like any mother, she prays for us and helps give us good things. Most important, she teaches us about her Son and helps us to be better followers of him.*

3 | review

Review this week's lesson by asking your child the following questions:

1. At the wedding in Cana, how did Mary help the young couple? (*Mary went to Jesus with their need.*)
2. What is the Assumption? (*Mary's being taken up, body and soul, into heaven at the end of her life.*)
3. What is an intercessor? (*One who prays for another.*)
4. What prayer most helps us know Mary and Jesus better? (*The Rosary.*)

References

- Student Textbook: Chapter 29, pp. 119–22
- Sacred Scripture: John 2:1–11; 19:26–27
- *Catechism of the Catholic Church*: 148–49, 490–93, 963–75, 2673–79, 2705–8

4 | apply

Help your child apply this week's lesson by asking the following questions:
1. Why do you think Mary's prayers for us are so powerful?
2. How do you think Mary can help you know and love Jesus better?
3. With what things can you ask Mary to help you? About what can you talk to her?

5 | conclude

- With your child, pray the Come, Holy Spirit prayer (see Appendix).

6 | follow up

During the week, do at least one of the following activities with your child:
1. Memorize John 2:5.
2. Make a book of the Mysteries of the Rosary (see Appendix). Beginning with the Joyful Mysteries, then the Luminous, the Sorrowful, and the Glorious, write the name of each mystery and an appropriate Scripture verse at the top of the page; then draw a picture of the event the mystery recalls.
3. Take flowers to the Marian altar or statue at your church and say a short prayer there.

His mother said to the servants, "Do whatever he tells you."
—John 2:5

notes

_____

_____

_____

_____

_____

_____

_____

Unto Everlasting Life

Lesson Focus | Everything in creation eventually dies, including us. When we die, our souls will be judged by God. If we die in friendship with God, with no sin on our souls, we will go to heaven. If we have small sins for which we still need to atone, we'll go to purgatory first. If we die in a state of serious sin, we will be making a choice to go to hell. At the end of time, the bodies of all the righteous will be reunited with their souls in heaven. There those people will know pure happiness, a joy greater than any on earth.

1 | begin

- Pray the Glory Be with your child.
- Tell your child about a loved one who died. Describe the person and tell your child about something fun you did together. Show him a picture if you have one. Then explain that, as sad as you are that the love one is no longer here, you hope to see him again in heaven.
- Read John 14:1–4 aloud.

2 | summarize

Summarize this week's lesson for your child:

Example: *Christ wants all his children to be with him in heaven. If we live good lives, striving for holiness, avoiding sin, and repenting for all we've done wrong, we'll be able to be with him and all those we loved who died loving him. We'll be happy forever in Heaven.*

References

- Student Textbook: Chapter 30, pp. 123–28

- Sacred Scripture: Mt 5:25–26, 31–46; Jn 14:1–4; Acts 1:9–11

- *Catechism of the Catholic Church*: 362–68, 946–62, 988–1041, 1720–24, 2012–16

3 | review

Review this week's lesson by asking your child the following questions:

1. What is the particular judgment? (*The judgment each individual person faces immediately after death.*)
2. What is the general judgment? (*The event at the end of the world, in which everyone's destiny will be made known to all.*)
3. What is heaven? (*The eternal state of joy in which souls are united with God forever.*)
4. What is hell? (*An eternal state of suffering in which souls are separated from God forever.*)
5. What is purgatory? (*Temporary suffering after death to remove venial sin from the soul.*)

4 | apply

Help your child apply this week's lesson by asking the following questions:
1. What do you think heaven will be like? What will it be better than?
2. Why do you think anyone would choose hell? How can you avoid making that choice?
3. What person who has died might need your prayers?

5 | conclude

- With your child, pray the Come, Holy Spirit prayer (see Appendix).

6 | follow up

During the week, do at least one of the following activities with your child:
1 Memorize John 14:1.
2. After family meals or after Grace before meals, remember to include a brief prayer for the faithful departed (see Appendix).
3. Stop by your parish to arrange to have a Mass said for your departed friends and relatives. Write the date down on the calendar, and attend the Mass as a family.

> *"Let not your hearts be troubled; believe in God, believe also in me."*
> —John 14:1

notes

_____

_____

_____

_____

_____

_____

_____

Following Christ

Grade 6

"And if you obey the voice of the LORD your God, being careful to do all his commandments which I command you this day, the LORD your God will set you high above all the nations of the earth."
Deuteronomy 28:1

God Gives Us the Law

Lesson Focus | To help his children know how to do good and avoid evil, God gave us the Ten Commandments, also called the "Decalogue" (Greek *deka*, ten + *logos*, a word or speech). He also gave us Jesus, who taught that obedience to the law requires love of God and neighbor. Finally, he gave us a conscience to help us know right from wrong in specific situations. To help us, however, our consciences must be formed according to God's law, Jesus' example, and Church teaching. Forming our consciences rightly and obeying God is how we show God we love him and how we find happiness.

1 | begin

- Pray the Glory Be with your child.
- Tell your child about a time when you made a bad choice and disobeyed God. Explain what consequences followed your choice and how you felt afterward.
- Read Genesis 3:1–19 aloud.

2 | summarize

Summarize this week's lesson for your child:

Example: *Although Adam and Eve knew right from wrong, they chose to disobey God. They didn't listen to his commandments or their consciences. When we sin, we do the same. The consequences of that are never good, because God's law is the only path to true happiness.*

3 | review

Review this week's lesson by asking your child the following questions:

1. What is another name for the Ten Commandments? (*The Decalogue.*)
2. What is the conscience? (*The faculty by which we judge whether an action is good or evil.*)
3. Why did God give us free will? (*So we can choose to love and follow him.*)
4. How did Jesus perfect the Ten Commandments? (*By giving us the Law of Love.*)
5. What are the Ten Commandments in order? (*See Appendix for full list.*)

References

- Student Textbook: Chapter 1, pp. 13–16

- Sacred Scripture: Gen 1:1—3:24; Ex 19—20:22; 24; 25:10–12, 31:19—32:35; Mt 5

- *Catechism of the Catholic Church*: 385–401, 574–82, 1776–89, 1961–74, 2070–74

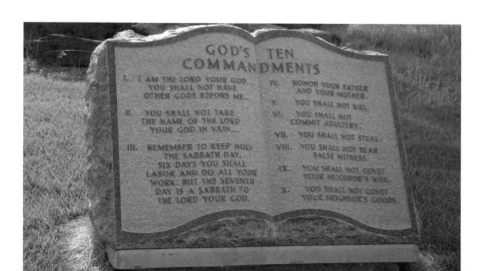

4 | apply

Help your child apply this week's lesson by asking the following questions:
1. Tell me about a time you did not listen to God's law or your conscience. How did you feel afterward? What were the consequences of your choice?
2. Tell me about a time you did listen to God's law and your conscience. How did you feel afterward? What were the consequences of that choice?
3. What are three things you can do every day to form your conscience rightly?

5 | conclude

- With your child, pray the Our Father.

6 | follow up

During the week, do at least one of the following activities with your child:
1. Memorize Matthew 5:8.
2. Have your child write a "Choose Your Own Adventure" story about a boy or girl who faced a difficult choice. Include two endings, one that tells what happened when a good choice was made and one that shows what happened when a bad choice was made.
3. In the morning before school, pray the Prayer to My Guardian Angel (see Appendix) together, and ask your guardian angels to help you make good choices that day. If, during the week, your child makes a bad choice, remind him to ask his guardian angel for help making good choices.

Blessed are the pure in heart, for they shall see God.
—Matthew 5:8

notes

_____

_____

_____

_____

_____

_____

_____

_____

The First Commandment in Our Own Day

Lesson Focus | The First Commandment teaches us that there is one true God and we are called to worship him. Superstition and impiety are ways we can violate this commandment. We can also do so by heresy, apostasy, and in other ways of rejecting the Church's teaching. We violate it when we put someone or something before God—when we give a created person or thing the kind of love and devotion that is due only to God. We honor this commandment when we worship God in the Holy Sacrifice of the Mass.

1 | begin

- Pray the Glory Be with your child.
- Ask your child how he would feel if you scheduled a special outing with him, then changed your mind at the last minute to watch a television show. What would he think?
- Read Mark 10:17–22 aloud.

2 | summarize

Summarize this week's lesson for your child:

Example: *If I canceled special plans with you, only to watch TV, I would be saying to you what the rich young man said to Jesus: something else is more important to me than you. But the First Commandment teaches that we must never say or act that way toward God. He must always come first.*

3 | review

Review this week's lesson by asking your child the following questions:

1. What does the First Commandment call us to do? (*To believe in, hope in, and love God above all else, and to worship him.*)
2. What is superstition? (*The belief that creatures and things have supernatural powers.*)
3. What is impiety? (*Lacking reverence or proper respect for God.*)
4. How are heresy and apostasy different? (*Heresy is the rejection of a teaching of the Faith and apostasy is a rejection of the Faith.*)
5. What is idolatry? (*The sin of worshipping something other than God.*)
6. What is detachment? (*Letting go of things when God asks it of us.*)

References

- Student Textbook: Chapter 2, pp. 17–20

- Sacred Scripture: Ex 32:1–28; Ps 139; Mt 6:24–30; Mk 10:17–22

- *Catechism of the Catholic Church*: 1356–81, 2084–2136, 2544–47

4 | apply

Help your child apply this week's lesson by asking the following questions:

1. What is an example of superstition? Impiety? Heresy?
2. Can you think of a time you've put something before God? When?
3. If we skip our prayers or Mass, what does that say to God? Why is that a problem?

5 | conclude

- With your child, pray the Our Father.

6 | follow up

During the week, do at least one of the following activities with your child:

1. Memorize Exodus 20:2–3.
2. Talk about things your child or your family does that might get in the way of evening or morning prayers (watching television too late, playing video games for too long, sleeping in, etc.). Resolve to give up that activity for one week, then do it less after the week is over.
3. As a family, go to Mass on one extra day this week.

> *I am the LORD your God, who brought you out of the land of Egypt, out of the house of bondage. You shall have no other gods before me.*
> —Exodus 20:2–3

notes

_____

_____

_____

_____

_____

_____

_____

_____

Prayer—Hidden Treasure

Lesson Focus | Obeying the First Commandment requires regular prayer. Prayer is the lifting of the heart and mind to God. It is a conversation with him, in which we thank him, praise him, tell him we're sorry for our sins, and ask for what we need. It's also a time to listen to him in our heart. Jesus encouraged his followers to pray always, trusting that God would always answer. The same is true for us. We must always pray, even when we're distracted or don't feel like praying. Without prayer, we can't fully love God or others.

1 | begin

- Pray the Glory Be with your child.
- Tell your child a little about your own prayer life. Share a story about a time prayer made a difference in your life or what your favorite prayer or favorite place to pray is.
- Together read Luke 18:1–8 aloud.

2 | summarize

Summarize this week's lesson for your child:

Example: *We can't love or worship God without prayer. Prayer is simply listening to God and talking to him —telling him our needs and that we love him, are sorry for our sins, and are grateful for his gifts.*

3 | review

Review this week's lesson by asking your child the following questions:
1. What is prayer? (*Raising the heart and mind to God; talking with God.*)
2. What is vocal prayer? (*Praying aloud, using either set formulas or our own words.*)
3. What is meditation? (*Praying using our mind, heart, and imagination to consider and seek the Lord and his will for us.*)
4. What is contemplation? (*Praying by being simply and lovingly united with God.*)
5. What prayer does Mary ask us to say every day? (*The Rosary.*)
6. What prayer did Jesus give us? (*The Our Father.*)
7. What is another name for the Liturgy of the Hours? (*The Divine Office.*)
8. Name the mysteries of the Rosary in order. (*See Appendix for full list*).

References

- Student Textbook: Chapter 3, pp. 21–24
- Sacred Scripture: Ps 139:4; Mt 6:8; 7:7–11; Lk 18:1–8
- *Catechism of the Catholic Church*: 2096–98, 2559–65, 2607–43, 2705–8, 2734–41

4 | apply

Help your child apply this week's lesson by asking the following questions:
1. Could you be friends with a person if you never talked with him? Why or why not? Do you think you can be friends with God and love him without talking with him?
2. Who is a saint you admire? How do you think prayer helped that person live a holy life and love others?
3. What can you do to overcome distractions during prayer?

5 | conclude

- With your child, pray the Our Father.

6 | follow up

During the week, do at least one of the following activities with your child:
1. Memorize Romans 12:15.
2. As a family, pray the evening or night prayers of the Liturgy of the Hours. All the prayers for each day are available online. You can also subscribe to *Magnificat* or *Magnifikids*, which feature the daily Scripture readings and abbreviated, family–friendly forms of the Divine Office.
3. Make a prayer board to help your family keep track of your prayer intentions and the intentions of others for whom you are praying.

Rejoice with those who rejoice, weep with those who weep.
—Romans 12:15

notes

Saints—They Made the Most of It

Lesson Focus | Every person was made to be in a close, personal relationship with God, and doing what we were made for is the key to happiness. That's why the saints are the happiest people of all. They are God's closest friends. They are also our friends, who intercede for us before God and teach us how to follow him better. Sainthood, however, isn't just for the few. God desires sainthood for all his children. We're all called to holiness and can never be truly happy until we attain it.

1 | begin

- Pray the Glory Be with your child.
- Tell your child who your favorite saint is and why, as well as what you've learned from him and how he has helped you. Show him the saint's picture if you can find one.
- Read Matthew 25:14–30 aloud.

2 | summarize

Summarize this week's lesson for your child:

Example: *The saints are like the good stewards. They wisely used all the gifts and graces God gave them to become holy, to become the people God made them to be. In heaven, they continue to use those gifts to help us. They are our friends, who teach us how to become saints too.*

3 | review

Review this week's lesson by asking your child the following questions:

1. What is the Church Triumphant? (*All the saints in heaven.*)
2. What is conversion? (*Turning away from sin and toward God.*)
3. What is intercession? (*Speaking up or praying for another person.*)
4. Do Catholics worship Mary and the saints? (*No, we worship God alone. We honor the saints and ask for their prayers. We honor and rely on Mary most of all, because she is the greatest of the saints and our Mother.*)
5. Are there more saints than just those who have been canonized? What is a saint? (*Yes; everyone who has died in friendship with God and has gone to heaven is a saint. We know the names of only a few.*)
6. When the Church declares someone to be a saint, can she be wrong? (*No.*)

References

- Student Textbook: Chapter 4, pp. 25–29

- Sacred Scripture: Mt 13:44–46; 25:14–30

- *Catechism of the Catholic Church*: 946–59, 1023–29, 2012–14, 2156, 2634–36, 2683–84

4 | apply

Help your child apply this week's lesson by asking the following questions:

1. Who is your patron saint and why? How can he or she help you?
2. Conversion is a lifelong process, something that happens every day, not just once. What can help you in this process of rejecting sin and choosing God?
3. What can you do every day that will help you become a saint?

5 | conclude

- With your child, pray the Our Father.

6 | follow up

During the week, do at least one of the following activities with your child:

1. Memorize 2 Timothy 4:7.
2. Find a book or movie for your child about the life of his patron saint or another favorite saint. Read or watch it together.
3. Search online for a novena to your child's patron saint or another favorite saint. Pick a special prayer intention, and say the novena together for nine days.

> *I have fought the good fight, I have finished the race, I have kept the faith.*
> *—2 Timothy 4:7*

notes

_____

_____

_____

_____

_____

_____

_____

The Holy Name

Lesson Focus | The Second Commandment teaches us always to respect God, his holy name, and holy things. To disrespect God's name by misusing it, swearing a casual or false oath by it, or speaking against it is a terrible thing to do to God, who gave his life for us. Out of love for God, the same respect should also be shown to holy things, such as the Bible, the vessels used in the Mass, religious statues and pictures, etc., as well as to persons who have consecrated their lives to God—priests, religious, consecrated singles, etc.

1 | begin

- Pray the Glory Be with your child.
- Show your child an item that's precious to you (e.g., a wedding ring, heirloom, treasured gift from a friend, etc.). Explain why it's important and how you care for it and protect it.
- Read Philippians 2:9–11 aloud.

2 | summarize

Summarize this week's lesson for your child:
Example: *Just as I show my love and gratitude for (name item from above) by taking good care of it, we're all called to show love and gratitude for God, who is so much more important than a thing, by always respecting his name and all the holy things that belong to him.*

References

- Student Textbook: Chapter 5, pp. 30–32

- Sacred Scripture: Gen 17:1–8; 32:24–30; Ex 3:1–10; 20:7; 1 Sam 3:1–10; Lk 19:2–6; Phil 2:9–11

- *Catechism of the Catholic Church*: 203–13, 1667–78, 2142–59

3 | review

Review this week's lesson by asking your child the following questions:
1. What does the Second Commandment call us to do? (*Respect the Lord's name.*)
2. In what ways can you show disrespect for God's name? (*Using it as a swear word, speaking against it, swearing false or casual oaths by it.*)
3. What other holy things does the Second Commandment call you to respect? (*The saints; people who give their lives to God, such as priests; objects used for Mass, and devotional items.*)
4. How should you respect God's name? (*Speak it with reverence; honor the vows sworn by it.*)
5. What is blasphemy? (*Speaking abusively or scornfully of God, the saints, and holy things.*)

4 | apply

Help your child apply this week's lesson by asking the following questions:

1. How would you feel if someone spoke badly about me or used my name as a swear word? Why should you feel the same way when someone uses God's name that way?
2. Have you ever used God's name in vain? Did you realize what you were doing? Why should you try hard never to do that again?
3. What are some ways you can show God you respect him and all that belongs to him?

5 | conclude

- With your child, pray the Apostles' Creed (see Appendix).

6 | follow up

During the week, do at least one of the following activities with your child:

1. Memorize Psalm 113:3.
2. Teach your child to venerate devotional items, such as crucifixes or relics, with a light kiss.
3. During Mass or when praying, bow your head slightly whenever Jesus' name is said.

From the rising of the sun to its setting the name of the Lord is to be praised!
—Psalm 113:3

notes

_____

_____

_____

_____

_____

_____

_____

_____

The Lord's Day

Lesson Focus | The Third Commandment instructs us to keep the Lord's Day holy. For Christians, the Lord's Day is Sunday because that is the day Christ rose from the dead. Keeping Sunday holy means avoiding unnecessary work, spending time with the people we love, and doing good for others. Above all, it means worshipping God with other Catholics in the Mass. God has given us so much, and in observing the Lord's Day, we give the gifts of ourselves and our time back to him. We also realize that all we have comes from him.

1 | begin

- Pray the Glory Be with your child.
- Tell your child about a special Sunday tradition you celebrated with your family as a child. Or share with him some of the things you thank God for every day.
- Read Genesis 2:1–3 aloud.

2 | summarize

Summarize this week's lesson for your child:

Example: *In Genesis 2, God teaches us to rest and worship on the Sabbath. We do those things to show our gratitude to him and to remember that some things are more important than work.*

3 | review

Review this week's lesson by asking your child the following questions:

1. What does the Third Commandment require us to do? (*Honor God on Sundays.*)
2. What does the Third Commandment say we must not do? (*Unnecessary work and activities that prevent us from honoring God in the Mass and getting the rest we need.*)
3. Is missing Mass, except for serious reasons, on Sundays and Holy Days of Obligation a mortal sin? (*Yes.*)
4. Why do we need to go to Mass? (*To worship and thank God publicly, as part of his Church, and to grow in grace as well as in faith. hope, and charity.*)
5. Why do we celebrate the Lord's Day on Sunday? (*Christ rose from the dead on Sunday.*)
6. What are the six Holy Days of obligation and their dates? (*Mary, Mother of God—January 1; Ascension—forty days after Easter; Assumption of Mary—August 15; All Saints—November 1; Immaculate Conception—December 8; Christmas—December 25.*)

References

- Student Textbook: Chapter 6, pp. 33–37

- Sacred Scripture: Gen 2:2; Mk 16:2; Acts 20:7

- *Catechism of the Catholic Church:* 2096–97, 2168–88

4 | apply

Help your child apply this week's lesson by asking the following questions:

1. What does our family do to make Sunday special? What else could we do?
2. Through the centuries and even today, Christians have risked their lives to go to Mass. Why do you think they've done that? Would you do that? Why or why not?
3. At Mass, how can you thank God for his gifts? What will you thank him for this Sunday?

5 | conclude

- With your child, pray the Our Father.

6 | follow up

During the week, do at least one of the following activities with your child:

1. Memorize Psalm 118:24.
2. Pick one special activity, in addition to attending Mass, that you can do as a family on Sunday. Try to do this every Sunday.
3. Learn about the underground Catholic Church in China and the men and women who have given up their lives or freedom trying to attend Mass.

This is the day which the LORD has made; let us rejoice and be glad in it.
—Psalm 118:24

notes

_____

_____

_____

_____

_____

_____

_____

The Cross and True Riches

Lesson Focus | Although Original Sin is washed away in Baptism, its effects still remain in us. The greatest of these lasting effects is a tendency to sin. The Church teaches us to practice self-denial to overcome this tendency. By denying ourselves in small things and bearing with patience the trials that come to us, we develop the moral strength and self-discipline to avoid sin and choose to do good. In this, we become imitators of Christ, who freely chose to submit to his Father's will and freely gave his life for us.

1 | begin

- Pray the Glory Be with your child.
- Tell your child about a sacrifice you've made for God—doing something that was difficult but right—and what good, both for you and others, came of that sacrifice.
- Read Philippians 2:1–16 aloud.

2 | summarize

Summarize this week's lesson for your child:

Example: *If we want to love God and others as we want to be loved, we must practice self-denial and accept God's will in all things. This is hard, but if we ask, God will help us to do it.*

3 | review

Review this week's lesson by asking your child the following questions:

1. What is self-denial? (*Giving up something we desire or doing something we do not desire for a higher purpose.*)
2. How did Jesus show his obedience to the Father? (*By dying on the Cross.*)
3. Does God ever allow us to suffer more than we can bear? (*No.*)
4. What is penance? (*Something done to make up for sin.*)
5. What are the two penitential seasons in the Church's liturgical year? (*Advent and Lent.*)
6. On what day of the week do Catholics practice voluntary penance? (*Friday.*)
7. What is the difference between fasting and abstinence? (*Fasting is eating less food than usual or no food at all. Abstinence is avoiding eating a certain food, such as meat.*)

References

- Student Textbook: Chapter 7, pp. 38–42
- Sacred Scripture: Phil 2:1–16; 1 Cor 9:24–27
- *Catechism of the Catholic Church*: 312, 524, 538–40, 606–18, 1430, 1434–39, 2339–42

4 | apply

Help your child apply this week's lesson by asking the following questions:

1. What is an example of a cross in your life that you haven't chosen? How has bearing it helped you to be a better, more loving person?
2. What is an example of a time you've denied yourself in the short term to achieve something important in the long term? Was it hard? Was the self-denial worth it? Why?
3. When you have to do something hard or something you don't want to do, how much do you complain? Name something you can try not to complain about in the future.

5 | conclude

- With your child, pray the Our Father.

6 | follow up

During the week, do at least one of the following activities with your child:

1. Memorize 2 Corinthians 9:7.
2. Evaluate how your family observes Friday penance. Do you observe it by giving up meat or doing some other act of penance? If not, resolve to do something together.
3. Pray for ten minutes in front of the crucifix in your church. Beforehand, talk to your child about what Jesus gave up for love of us, and ask him to pray about what he can give up for love of Jesus.

> *Each one must do as he has made up his mind, not reluctantly or under compulsion, for God loves a cheerful giver.*
> —2 Corinthians 9:7

notes

_____

_____

_____

_____

_____

_____

_____

In the Heart of the Family

Lesson Focus | The Fourth Commandment teaches us to honor our father and mother. We owe them this honor because they have given us the gift of life, as well as their love and care. When we are young, we honor our parents by loving and obeying them. As we become adults, we honor them by loving them, listening to their advice, and caring for them in their old age. Even as we discover our parents' faults, we must continue to love them and help them.

1 | begin

- Pray the Glory Be with your child.
- Share with your child a favorite childhood memory of your parents — something special you did together or something they did that made you feel safe and loved.
- Read Luke 2:41–52 aloud.

2 | summarize

Summarize this week's lesson for your child:

Example: *Jesus gave us the perfect example of how to obey the Fourth Commandment: honoring his parents by obeying them, as well as loving, trusting, and caring for them.*

3 | review

Review this week's lesson by asking your child the following questions:

1. What does the Fourth Commandment call us to do? (*Honor our father and mother; respect those in authority.*)
2. What does it mean to honor someone? (*To hold him in high regard, to respect him, and to love him.*)
3. To whom besides our parents did God give authority over us? (*Teachers, civil authorities, babysitters, coaches, etc.*)
4. How can we honor our parents? (*By obeying them, loving them, listening to them, not keeping secrets from them, taking care of them as they grow old, etc.*)
5. How can we help our parents grow in holiness? (*By praying for them, making sacrifices for them, sharing with them what we know and learn, etc.*)
6. What did Blessed John Paul II say must be the main target of the renewal of society? (*Strengthening family life.*)

References

- Student Textbook: Chapter 8, pp. 43–45

- Sacred Scripture: Ex 20:12; Lk 2:41–52

- *Catechism of the Catholic Church*: 2099–2100, 1655–58, 2197–2246, 2634–36

4 | apply

Help your child apply this week's lesson by asking the following questions:

1. Can you give an example of a way in which you've honored me?
2. Can you give an example of a time you've failed to honor me?
3. What is something we both can do to honor each other?

5 | conclude

- With your child, pray the Our Father.

6 | follow up

During the week, do at least one of the following activities with your child:

1. Memorize Romans 12:10.
2. Plan a special evening or afternoon out with your child. Go to lunch, to dinner, to a game, or shopping, and talk about what is going on with your child's school, sports, or friends.
3. Place a picture of the Holy Family somewhere in your home where you will see it every day. If possible, put it in a place where you say morning or evening prayers together.

Love one another with brotherly affection; outdo one another in showing honor.
—Romans 12:10

notes

_____

_____

_____

_____

_____

_____

_____

_____

Citizenship—Rights and Duties

Lesson Focus | In order for all men to coexist peacefully, God has entrusted civil authorities—the government—with the power to make laws for its citizens. There are many types of government, but all are obliged to pass laws that are just and good and in accord with God's laws. As citizens, we are obliged to obey the laws, pay taxes, and defend our nation. As Christians, we're obliged to work to change unjust laws and build a civil society that cares for, respects, and protects the lives of all human beings. Citizens of strong nations are obliged to help poor and oppressed people of other nations.

1 | begin

- Pray the Glory Be with your child.
- Show your child a picture of the president. Remind him that the Church prays for the president at Sunday Mass during the Prayers of the Faithful. Ask him why he thinks the Church does this.
- Read Matthew 22:17–21 aloud.

2 | summarize

Summarize this week's lesson for your child:

Example: *God wants us all to be good citizens and Christians—obeying rightful authorities and the laws of our land, but also working to make sure that those laws are right and just.*

3 | review

Review this week's lesson by asking your child the following questions:

1. What authority does the state have? (*The authority to make just laws.*)
2. From whom does that authority come? (*God.*)
3. What is patriotism? (*Love of one's country.*)
4. As Catholics, what must we do if the civil authorities command us to do something that violates God's law? (*We must obey God, not the state.*)
5. If something is legal, is it therefore moral? (*No.*)

References

- Student Textbook: Chapter 9, pp. 46–49

- Sacred Scripture: Mt 22:17–21; 28:18–20; Mk 10:2–9; Jn 19:1–8

- *Catechism of the Catholic Church*: 1897–99, 1918–21, 2234–46, 2270–75, 2420–25, 2436

4 | apply

Help your child apply this week's lesson by asking the following questions:

1. How can the government be a force for good in the world? Give an example.
2. How can the government be a force for evil, misusing its authority? Give an example.
3. What are three things you personally can do to help build a good and just society?

5 | conclude

- With your child, pray the Our Father.

6 | follow up

During the week, do at least one of the following activities with your child:

1. Memorize Romans 13:1.
2. As a family watch the movie *A Man for All Seasons* about Saint Thomas More.
3. As a family, pray a Rosary (or a decade of the Rosary) for the president and other elected officials.

Let every person be subject to the governing authorities. For there is no authority except from God, and those that exist have been instituted by God.
—Romans 13:1

notes

_____

_____

_____

_____

_____

_____

_____

Church Authority—Our Fathers in Faith

Lesson Focus | The Church derives her authority from Jesus, who founded her so that all men might know Him and be saved. The Pope is the visible head of the Church on earth. He is called the "Vicar of Christ" because he acts for and in the place of Jesus. The bishop is the head of a diocese. Together, the Pope and bishops safeguard Christ's teachings. To ensure that the Faith is taught correctly and that the Sacraments are celebrated properly, The Pope and the bishops have the authority to establish laws about those matters. We show our love for Christ when we respect and obey their authority.

1 | begin

- Pray the Glory Be with your child.
- Search online for a recent news story about the Pope. Read it together with your child.
- Read Matthew 16:13–20 aloud.

2 | summarize

Summarize this week's lesson for your child:

Example: *Christ entrusted the authority to lead, rule, and guide his Church to Saint Peter, the Apostles, and all the Popes and bishops who have followed them. They are our fathers in faith.*

3 | review

References

- Student Textbook: Chapter 10, pp. 50–53

- Sacred Scripture: Mt 16:13–20; Jn 14:16–17; 15:26–27; 16:13; 21:14–19; 1 Jn 4:6

- *Catechism of the Catholic Church*: 77–79, 758–69, 813–22, 857–65, 871–96

Review this week's lesson by asking your child the following questions:

1. Who is the Vicar of Christ and why does he have that title? (*The Pope is called the Vicar of Christ because he acts on Christ's behalf with Christ's authority.*)
2. What is the Magisterium and what are its duties? (*The Pope and all the bishops together in union with him; to interpret Sacred Scripture and Sacred Tradition.*)
3. What is infallibility? (*The protection granted by the Holy Spirit to the Church's Magisterium that keeps her teachings on faith and morals free from error.*)
4. Name the precepts of the Church. (*1. Attend Mass on Sundays and Holy Days; 2. Confess sins at least once a year; 3. Receive the Eucharist during the Easter season; 4. Observe the Church's days of fasting and abstinence; 5. Provide for the Church's needs.*)

4 | apply

Help your child apply this week's lesson by asking the following questions:
1. How is the Church like a mother?
2. How does the authority exercised by the Church help you know and love Jesus?
3. How can you show your love for the Church and her authority?

5 | conclude

- With your child, pray the Our Father.

6 | follow up

During the week, do at least one of the following activities with your child:
1. Memorize Luke 10:16.
2. Online, learn more about Saint Peter—his life after Jesus' Ascension, his journey to Rome, and his martyrdom.
3. Look up online the Pope's prayer intentions for the month. Pray for those intentions daily.

He who hears you hears me, and he who rejects you rejects me, and he who rejects me rejects him who sent me.
—Luke 10:16

notes

_____

_____

_____

_____

_____

_____

_____

Respect Life

Lesson Focus | The Fifth Commandment teaches us that we must never take an innocent life. We must protect life from the moment a child is conceived in his mother's womb until natural death. Abortion and euthanasia are grave moral evils, as wrong as murder. Even when killing someone is permissible—in self-defense, a just war, or as capital punishment—it is still a serious matter and must not be taken lightly. Failing to care for our bodies, being reckless about others' safety, and committing suicide also violate this commandment.

1 | begin

- Pray the Glory Be with your child.
- Tell your child about when you were (or your wife was) pregnant with him. Tell him how he moved, what you would talk to him about, and how much you loved him.
- Read Genesis 1:26–31 aloud.

2 | summarize

Summarize this week's lesson for your child:

Example: *Because we are all made in God's image, every human life is sacred and we must always respect our own life and the lives of others by never depriving any innocent person of that gift.*

3 | review

Review this week's lesson by asking your child the following questions:
1. As human beings, we are a union of _____ and _____. (*Body and soul.*)
2. What does the Fifth Commandment forbid? (*Directly and intentionally taking an innocent life.*)
3. Why is abortion wrong? (*Because it destroys the life of the unborn child, who is a human person from the moment of conception.*)
4. What is euthanasia? (*Taking the life of someone who is elderly or sick.*)
5. What things can we do to our own bodies that violate the Fifth Commandment? (*Commit suicide, eat too much, drink too much alcohol, abuse drugs.*)
6. Under what serious circumstances is it not morally wrong to kill someone? (*When we act in self-defense, in a just war, or in a just use of capital punishment.*)

References

- Student Textbook: Chapter 11, pp. 54–56
- Sacred Scripture: Gen 1:26–31, 2:4–25
- *Catechism of the Catholic Church*: 362–68, 2258–2317

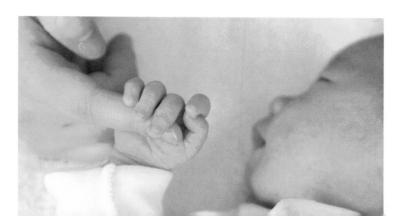

4 | apply

Help your child apply this week's lesson by asking the following questions:
1. What should you do to take care of yourself?
2. What is something you can do to help end abortion?
3. How can you show God that you respect all life?

5 | conclude

- With your child, pray the Our Father.

6 | follow up

During the week, do at least one of the following activities with your child:
1. Memorize Psalm 139:13.
2. Find a regular time each day for your child to get at least thirty minutes of exercise.
3. Pray a Rosary or Divine Mercy Chaplet (see Appendix) for an end to abortion. If there is an abortion facility nearby, consider praying the Rosary outside the clinic on a Saturday.

For you formed my inward parts, you knitted me together in my mother's womb.
—Psalm 139:13

notes

_____
_____
_____
_____
_____
_____
_____
_____

Charity toward All

Lesson Focus | The Fifth Commandment also tells us we must never harm another person's soul by hating him, through acts of anger, or by causing others to sin. Instead, as we are told by Jesus, we must love even our enemies. This doesn't mean we have to feel love for them. Rather, it means we must always will their good and never do anything to harm them. Although anger can be just, we must never let our anger lead us into sin.

1 | begin

- Pray the Glory Be with your child.
- Tell your child about a time you forgave someone who hurt you. Tell him whether it was hard to forgive that person and how you felt after you forgave him.
- Read Luke 6:27–35 aloud.

2 | summarize

Summarize this week's lesson for your child:

Example: *To be cruel to another person or to seek to hurt anyone, even those who hurt us, is always wrong. No matter what a person has done, we must forgive him and pray for him.*

3 | review

Review this week's lesson by asking your child the following questions:

1. Whom must we love? (*Both our friends and our enemies.*)
2. What is the sin of scandal? (*Leading others to sin by our words or example.*)
3. Can anger ever be righteous or just? (*Yes.*)
4. May we ever seek vengeance on those who've hurt us? (*No.*)
5. What does it mean to hate someone? As Christians are we allowed to hate anyone? (*To want bad things to happen to him; no.*)

References

- Student Textbook: Chapter 12, pp. 57–60

- Sacred Scripture: Mt 5:22–25; 18:6; Lk 6:27–35; 10:30–37; Jn 2:13–17; Rom 7:14–25

- *Catechism of the Catholic Church*: 743, 1813, 1822–39, 2284–87, 2302–3, 2842–45

4 | apply

Help your child apply this week's lesson by asking the following questions:

1. Have you ever hurt a person out of anger? Who? Have you asked for his forgiveness?
2. Who has hurt you out of anger? Have you forgiven him? How would forgiving help you?
3. Write out the Corporal and Spiritual Works of mercy (see Appendix), and, next to each, list one example of how you could perform that work of mercy.

5 | conclude

- With your child, pray the Our Father.

6 | follow up

During the week, do at least one of the following activities with your child:

1. Memorize 1 John 3:15.
2. From the list of examples from Step 4, pick one Corporal Work of Mercy and one Spiritual Work of Mercy to do together as a family this week.
3. Learn about the assassination attempt on Blessed John Paul II in 1981 and how he treated the man who shot him, Mehmet Ali Agca.

Everyone who hates his brother is a murderer, and you know that no murderer has eternal life remaining in him.
—1 John 3:15

notes

_____

_____

_____

_____

_____

_____

_____

The Sacred Flame

Lesson Focus | The Sixth and Ninth Commandments instruct us to respect our own and others' dignity in both our actions and thoughts. One of the most important ways we do this is by respecting God's plan for marriage, family life, and sexuality. That means developing the virtue of self-control so we can live the virtue of chastity, using the gift of our sexuality only in marriage, and using it only as God asks us to use it. This gift is a precious one and can easily be abused, so we must guard it, understand it, and use it wisely.

1 | begin

- Pray the Glory Be with your child.
- Ask your child how he images his Father, God. How is he like God? Possible answers: in his ability to love, to choose right from wrong, to reason, etc.
- Read Genesis 2:15–25 aloud.

2 | summarize

Summarize this week's lesson for your child:

Example: *Of all the ways we image God, the most important is our ability to give ourselves, in love, to another and, in that giving, partner with God in creating new life. That ability is a precious gift, and we respect that gift by respecting God's plan for human love and sexuality.*

3 | review

Review this week's lesson by asking your child the following questions:

1. What two commandments teach us to guard the gift of sexuality? (*The sixth and ninth.*)
2. Does using self-control and following the Sixth and Ninth Commandments take away our freedom? (*No. Self-control, like any virtue, helps us to do freely what is good for ourselves and for others.*)
3. To respect our own and others' dignity, what does God require of us? (*Chastity and purity of heart.*)
4. What does God do for us when we choose to follow his plan for sexuality? (*He gives us the grace we need to follow that plan.*)

References

- Student Textbook: Chapter 13, pp. 61–64
- Sacred Scripture: Gen 1:26 – 2:25; 1 Cor 6:19
- *Catechism of the Catholic Church*: 1700–12, 1934–38, 2284–2301, 2331–91, 2514–27

4 | apply

Help your child apply this week's lesson by asking the following questions:
1. To avoid sins against chastity and purity, what else should you avoid?
2. Self-control helps us avoid sins against chastity. How can you develop that virtue?
3. In what ways can going against God's plan for human sexuality hurt you? How could it hurt another person?

5 | conclude

- With your child, pray the Our Father.

6 | follow up

During the week, do at least one of the following activities with your child:
1. Memorize 1 Corinthians 6:19.
2. When you see a depiction of unchastity—such as a suggestive ad—say, "Isn't it sad that the makers of that ad don't understand how precious they are to God? We should pray for them."
3. Make a point over the next several weeks of watching television with your child. If anything in the program encourages or depicts sins against chastity or purity, discuss those scenes with your child. Ask him what he thinks about the choices made and why they are problematic. Point out what consequences might or did follow the actions. Decide whether or not watching that program in the future is good for your family.

Do you not know that your body is a temple of the Holy Spirit within you, which you have from God? You are not your own.
—1 Corinthians 6:19

notes

_____

_____

_____

_____

_____

_____

_____

Ownership

Lesson Focus | The Seventh and Tenth Commandments teach us to respect our own property and the property of others. We respect others' property by never taking what isn't ours, by caring for what we've borrowed, and by making restitution when we damage someone else's property. We respect our own property by being grateful for what we have, caring for it, giving generously to those in need, and not being envious of those who have more.

1 | begin

- Pray the Glory Be with your child.
- Tell your child about a time someone damaged or stole something of yours. How did it affect you? What problems did it cause? Did the person make restitution?
- Read Matthew 25:34–40 aloud.

2 | summarize

Summarize this week's lesson for your child:

Example: *God gives us property so we can be safe, healthy, and happy. But he never wants us to care about things more than we care about helping others or about him. He calls us to be thankful for what we have, to share with others, and always to respect what belongs to others.*

3 | review

Review this week's lesson by asking your child the following questions:

1. What does the Seventh Commandment call us to do? (*To respect our own property and the property of others.*)
2. What are ways you can violate the Seventh Commandment? (*Theft — taking what isn't yours; fraud — deceiving someone in order to take what is his; usury — charging excessive interest on a loan.*)
3. Is cheating on a test or copying someone's else's work theft? (*Yes.*)
4. What is restitution? (*Making up for what has been stolen, damaged, or destroyed.*)
5. What does the Tenth Commandment call us to do? (*To be happy with what we have and what we do not have, and to be happy with another's success.*)
6. What is envy? (*Being saddened by another's success or good fortune.*)
7. What is avarice? (*Excessive desire for wealth and things; greed.*)

References

- Student Textbook: Chapter 14, pp. 65–68
- Sacred Scripture: Mt 25:34–40
- *Catechism of the Catholic Church*: 1822–29, 2401–49, 2534–50

4 | apply

Help your child apply this week's lesson by asking the following questions:

1. Has anyone ever damaged or taken something of yours? How did that make you feel?
2. Think of someone you know who is very generous with everything he has. How is he generous?
3. On a scale of 1 to 10, with 10 being the best, rate yourself as a steward of all that God has given you. What could you do to be a better steward?

5 | conclude

- With your child, pray the Our Father.

6 | follow up

During the week, do at least one of the following activities with your child:

1. Memorize Hebrews 13:16.
2. Encourage your child to begin saving ten percent of his allowance or the money he earns to give to a charity that helps the poor and the needy.
3. During evening prayers, have everyone in the family tell God for what he is thankful.

Do not neglect to do good and to share what you have, for such sacrifices are pleasing to God.
—Hebrews 13:16

notes

_____

_____

_____

_____

_____

_____

_____

Backed by Truth

Lesson Focus | The Eighth Commandment calls us to use our power of speech for the good. That means always telling the truth. It also means not speaking ill of others, repeating gossip, or revealing a secret that is not ours to reveal. Finally, it means honoring our promises and oaths and living lives that are consistent with the truth we claim to believe.

1 | begin

- Pray the Glory Be with your child.
- Tell your child about a time you either didn't tell the truth or were hurt when someone else didn't tell the truth. Explain why the lie was told, the consequences, and how the lie was discovered. Make a point of showing how many people were hurt by it.
- Together read James 3:2–12 aloud.

2 | summarize

Summarize this week's lesson for your child:

Example: *James says that our words have great power. When used rightly, they can be a force for good. But when used wrongly, they can cause great harm.*

3 | review

Review this week's lesson by asking your child the following questions:

1. What does the Eighth Commandment call us to do? (*To use speech for good purposes; to speak the truth.*)
2. Explain the difference between slander and detraction. (*Slander is saying something harmful about someone that's false; detraction is saying something harmful that's true.*)
3. What is gossip? (*Idle or malicious talk about others.*)
4. What is rumor? (*Spreading a story you do not know to be true.*)
5. What is the difference between false witness and perjury? (*False witness is the sin of giving untrue testimony or lying about another. Perjury is lying under oath.*)
6. Can speaking the truth be sinful? How? (*Yes, sometimes it's better not to point out a person's faults because doing so might be hurtful.*)
7. What is rash judgment? (*Judging another's behavior to be wrong without enough evidence.*)

References

- Student Textbook: Chapter 15, pp. 69–72

- Sacred Scripture: Mt 5:10–11; 12:36–37; Jn 1:1–14; 4:24; 14:6; 1 Cor 13:6–7; Eph 4:29; Jas 3:2–12

- *Catechism of the Catholic Church*: 2464–2503

4 | apply

Help your child apply this week's lesson by asking the following questions:

1. Give me an example of each of the following sins against the Eighth Commandment: slander, detraction, gossip, rumor, false witness, flattery, hypocrisy, rash judgment.
2. Choose three of the examples above. Whom do those sins hurt, and what consequences could follow?
3. Why do you think people speak badly about one another, gossiping and repeating rumors? If we love Jesus, why should we never commit those sins?

5 | conclude

- With your child, pray the Our Father.

6 | follow up

During the week, do at least one of the following activities with your child:

1. Memorize Ephesians 4:25.
2. As a family, pray the Prayer of Saint Patrick's Breastplate (see Appendix).
3. Visit your parish's Adoration Chapel or tabernacle. Spend fifteen to twenty minutes there in prayer, reflecting on the ways false words and accusations were used against Christ.

Therefore, putting away falsehood, let every one speak the truth with his neighbor, for we are members one of another.
—Ephesians 4:25

notes

_____

_____

_____

_____

_____

_____

_____

The Beatitudes

Lesson Focus | The Ten Commandments are known for teaching us what we should not do, but the Beatitudes teach us what we should do. Given to us by Christ during his Sermon on the Mount, they are the fulfillment (or the perfection) of the Old Law. In many ways, they also turn the laws of the world upside down. They tell us that the meek, the humble, the poor, and those who mourn are the ones who will find true happiness. This can seem impossible, but with God's grace, nothing is impossible.

1 | begin

- Pray the Glory Be with your child.
- Review your family's "Don't" rules: don't hit your siblings, don't talk back, etc. Then review the "Do" rules: Do be kind, do help one another, etc. Ask your child if your family could be happy with only "Don't" rules and no "Do" rules.
- Read Matthew 5:1–12 aloud.

2 | summarize

Summarize this week's lesson for your child:

Example: *The Ten Commandments contain "Don't" rules. They help us lead a good life. But to be truly happy and holy, we also need "Do" rules. That's why Jesus gave us the Beatitudes.*

3 | review

Review this week's lesson by asking your child the following questions:
1. How can we become poor in spirit? (*By not valuing things more than we value God and his will.*)
2. When we mourn, what must we do? (*Trust that God will comfort and strengthen us.*)
3. For what does Christ call us to hunger? (*Righteousness.*)
4. Why should we be merciful? (*Because we too are in need of mercy.*)
5. Who does Jesus promise will see God? (*The pure in heart.*)
6. If we are meek—humble and kind—what will we inherit? (*The Kingdom of God.*)
7. What will those who make peace be called? (*Sons of God.*)

References

- Student Textbook: Chapter 16, pp. 73–76
- Sacred Scripture: Mt 3:4–17; 5—7; Lk 6:20–23
- *Catechism of the Catholic Church*: 574–82, 1023–29, 1716–24, 2051–55, 2842–45

4 | apply

Help your child apply this week's lesson by asking the following questions:

1. Give an example of how you can practice each of the eight Beatitudes (see Matthew 5:1–12 for a complete list).
2. Tell me about a time you practiced one of the Beatitudes. Was it hard to do? How did you feel afterward?
3. What are some of the obstacles that make living the Beatitudes and the Christian life hard? How do you think you can overcome those obstacles? Why is it worth the effort?

5 | conclude

- With your child, pray the Our Father.

6 | follow up

During the week, do at least one of the following activities with your child:

1. Memorize Psalm 84:12.
2. Research Dorothy Day and learn how, as a modern laywoman, she strove to live the Beatitudes.
3. As a family, pray the Prayer of Saint Francis (see Appendix).

O LORD of hosts, blessed is the man who trusts in you!
—Psalm 84:12

notes

_____

_____

_____

_____

_____

_____

_____

At the Last Supper

Lesson Focus | At the Last Supper, Jesus instituted the Sacrament of the Eucharist: he changed bread and wine into his Body and Blood and commanded the Apostles to do the same in memory of him. At the Last Supper, a celebration of the Passover meal, Jesus instituted a new Passover, with himself as the sacrificial Lamb. In the Eucharist, the sacrifice Christ made on the Cross is both re-presented and recalled in his Church throughout time. Through it, the benefits and graces Christ won on the Cross are applied to those who receive the Eucharist.

1 | begin

- Pray the Glory Be with your child.
- Ask your child what are the most important gifts parents can give to their children. Answers might include: time, presence, love, life, an education, faith, virtue, etc.
- Read John 6:27–58 aloud.

2 | summarize

Summarize this week's lesson for your child:

Example: *At the Last Supper, Jesus instituted the Sacrament of the Eucharist, making possible what he spoke about in that passage from John's Gospel. Through the Eucharist, Jesus is with us always, giving us his own life so that we can love as he wants us to love.*

References

- Student Textbook: Chapter 17, pp. 79–82

- Sacred Scripture: Gen 4:1–12; 8:15–22; 22:1–18; Ex 12:1–14; Mt 26:17–30; Jn 1:29; 6:1–54

- *Catechism of the Catholic Church*: 128–30, 606–18, 1333–44, 1373–1401

3 | review

Review this week's lesson by asking your child the following questions:

1. What did Jesus say we must do to have eternal life? (*Eat his Flesh and drink his Blood.*)
2. When do we do that? (*Whenever we receive Holy Communion.*)
3. Who has the power to make that possible, and from where does that power come? (*Priests; from Christ through the Sacrament of Holy Orders.*)
4. What changes during the Consecration: the appearance of the matter or the substance? (*The appearance is still bread and wine, but the substance changes into Jesus' Body and Blood.*)
5. What graces do we receive at every Mass? (*The graces won for us by Christ on Calvary.*)

4 | apply

Help your child apply this week's lesson by asking the following questions:

1. After Jesus told his followers what they had to do to inherit eternal life, many walked away. Why do you think they did so? What would you have done?
2. Do you think the graces of the Eucharist help you love God and others better? How?
3. What can you do to show God greater appreciation for the gift of the Eucharist?

5 | conclude

- With your child, pray the Our Father.

6 | follow up

During the week, do at least one of the following activities with your child:

1. Memorize John 6:54.
2. After Mass, spend a few extra minutes giving thanks for the gift of the Eucharist.
3. During the week, visit your parish's Adoration Chapel or tabernacle for some quiet prayer. Encourage your child to bring a journal or a sketchpad as a prayer tool, using it to write out or draw for Jesus what's in his heart.

> *He who eats my flesh and drinks my blood has eternal life, and I will raise him up at the last day.*
> *—John 6:54*

notes

_____

_____

_____

_____

_____

_____

_____

The Living Sacrifice

Lesson Focus | The Mass is the re-presentation of Christ's one perfect sacrifice on Calvary. It is a memorial that makes present to us throughout time both his death and Resurrection. It is also a prayer. As a prayer, it allows us to worship God, to thank him for his good gifts, to atone for our sins through Christ's sacrifice on Calvary, and to place our prayers of petition, both for our own needs and the needs of others, before Christ.

1 | begin

- Pray the Glory Be with your child.
- Tell your child a little bit about what you pray about and for during the Mass. What praise do you offer? For what do you thank God? For what do you tell God you're sorry? For what do you ask?
- Read John 18:1–37 aloud.

2 | summarize

Summarize this week's lesson for your child:

Example: *At every Mass, we not only remember those events; we actually participate in them. Through the Mass, Jesus' sacrifice on the Cross is made present to us. That's why the Mass is both the perfect sacrifice and the perfect prayer. It is the best way we can worship God.*

3 | review

Review this week's lesson by asking your child the following questions:

1. In what way is Jesus a mediator? (*He bridges the gap between man and God, reconciling us to God and restoring our friendship with him by buying us back from sin.*)
2. How is the Mass a sacrifice? (*It is the sacrifice of Christ Himself on Calvary, re-presented.*)
3. Of what is it a memorial? (*Christ's death and Resurrection.*)
4. What are the four ends of the Mass? (*Worship, thanksgiving, satisfaction for sins, reception of graces.*)

References

- Student Textbook: Chapter 18, pp. 83–85
- Sacred Scripture: Jn 18:1 – 19:42
- *Catechism of the Catholic Church*: 606–18, 1341–81, 1459–60, 2099–2100, 2177–79

4 | apply

Help your child apply this week's lesson by asking the following questions:

1. If you were to offer a prayer of adoration in your own words, what would you say?
2. For what are you most especially grateful to God?
3. What special prayers of supplication do you want to bring before God right now? With what do you especially want his help?
4. If you were on Calvary with Jesus, what would you say to him? Do you think you should say those same things to him during the Mass? Why or why not?

5 | conclude

- With your child, pray the Our Father.

6 | follow up

During the week, do at least one of the following activities with your child:

1. Memorize Ephesians 5:2.
2. On Saturday, encourage your child to write down the things for which he wants to praise God, thank God, and ask God, as well as anything he wants to tell God he's sorry for, at Sunday Mass.
3. After Mass, as a family, say a short prayer in front of your Church's main crucifix or in front of a stained-glass window or Station of the Cross that depicts the Crucifixion.

And walk in love, as Christ loved us and gave himself up for us, a fragrant offering and sacrifice to God.

—Ephesians 5:2

notes

_____

_____

_____

_____

_____

_____

_____

_____

The Feast of God

Lesson Focus | Just as the Mass is a holy sacrifice, it is also a sacred meal, in which we receive "our daily bread," the Eucharist, food for our souls. It nourishes us spiritually, strengthening us in virtue and drawing us closer to Christ. It is his Body that we eat and his Blood that we drink, so it is his life we take into ourselves. We participate in this Sacred Meal, with our family, the Body of Christ, and should always show great reverence for it.

1 | begin

- Pray the Glory Be with your child.
- Search online for paintings of the Last Supper. Ask your child in what ways the Last Supper looks like a normal meal shared by friends. In what ways does it look different?
- Read Matthew 26:17–30 aloud.

2 | summarize

Summarize this week's lesson for your child:

Example: *The Last Supper was a sacred meal, where Jesus gave his Body and Blood to his disciples to eat and drink. In the same way, the Mass is a sacred meal, where we too receive Jesus' Body and Blood to eat and drink.*

3 | review

Review this week's lesson by asking your child the following questions:

1. In what ways is the Mass a banquet? (*The Mass is a family celebration with a feast, a Passover meal, the meal that completes the sacrifice. We consume spiritual food—Jesus.*)
2. What is our "daily bread"? (*God's providing for our needs each day; also, Christ is our daily bread, the spiritual bread of the Eucharist.*)
3. How is the Eucharist food for our souls? (*Just as normal food nourishes our body, the Eucharist nourishes our souls, strengthening and renewing the graces of our Baptism.*)
4. Why is receiving Communion so very special? (*Because of the one we receive—Christ himself.*)

References

- Student Textbook: Chapter 19, pp. 86–89

- Sacred Scripture: Mt 26:17–30; Mk 14:13–26; Lk 22:11–22; Jn 6:35–54; 1 Cor 11:23–26

- *Catechism of the Catholic Church*: 787–96, 1328–32, 1355, 1373–1401, 2837

4 | apply

Help your child apply this week's lesson by asking the following questions:

1. Before Mass, what can you do to prepare your heart to receive Jesus?
2. What gifts has God given you? Do you think any of those gifts is greater than his own Body, his own life? Why or why not?
3. Both during and after Mass, how can you show God that you recognize and are thankful for the gift of the Eucharist?

5 | conclude

- With your child, pray the Our Father.

6 | follow up

During the week, do at least one of the following activities with your child:

1. Memorize John 15:13.
2. On Sunday arrive at your parish at least five minutes early to pray before Mass begins.
3. Pick one night during the week, ideally Sunday, to have a special family meal with good food, a tablecloth, candles, and your best dishes. Invite family, godparents, or friends to share it with you. Before dinner, give special thanks to God for his gifts.

> *Greater love has no man than this, that a man lay down his life for his friends.*
> *—John 15:13*

notes

_____

_____

_____

_____

_____

_____

_____

Promise and Fulfillment

Lesson Focus | In the Gospel of John, Christ made it very clear that the Eucharist is not just a symbol of his Body and Blood. It is his Body and Blood. In the beginning, that teaching cost him many of his followers. It's still hard for many people to believe. But it remains true. Only because the Eucharist is truly Christ's Body and Blood can it do what it does—nourish us spiritually and conform us more and more to his likeness. As such, we must take great care to defend this truth and always receive the Eucharist worthily.

1 | begin

- Pray the Glory Be with your child.
- Show your child a treasured possession or family heirloom. Ask him how he would take care of it if you gave it to him. What would he do? What would he not do? Why?
- Read 1 Corinthians 11:26–29 aloud.

2 | summarize

Summarize this week's lesson for your child:

Example: *The Eucharist is the most precious gift God gives us. It is really and truly Christ's Body and Blood. It's the gift of his own life. That's why we must treasure it and always receive it with great reverence and respect.*

References

- Student Textbook: Chapter 20, pp. 90–92

- Sacred Scripture: Mt 28:16–20; Mk 14:22–24; Jn 6:35–69; 14:15–21; 1 Cor 11:26–29

- *Catechism of the Catholic Church*: 362–68, 441–45, 543–50, 1355, 1373–1401, 2837

3 | review

Review this week's lesson by asking your child the following questions:

1. How do we know that the Eucharist is truly Jesus' Body and Blood? (*Because he told us very clearly that it is.*)
2. When Jesus said, "My flesh is food"—difficult words to hear—why did Peter and the Apostles stay with him? (*Because they already believed that Jesus was the Messiah.*)
3. How do we know this is a hard teaching for some people to believe? (*Because many followers left Jesus when he taught it, and many people today still don't believe.*)
4. Can people who aren't Catholic receive the Eucharist? (*No.*)

4 | apply

Help your child apply this week's lesson by asking the following questions:
1. What can you do before or during Mass to increase the personal graces of Communion?
2. What could you do that would limit the personal graces of Communion?
3. If you were telling a friend why the Eucharist is important to you, what would you say?

5 | conclude

- With your child, pray the Our Father.

6 | follow up

During the week, do at least one of the following activities with your child:
1. Memorize 1 Corinthians 11:29.
2. Before you receive Communion, bow or genuflect out of respect for Christ.
3. As a family, go to confession this week.

For any one who eats and drinks without discerning the body eats and drinks judgment upon himself.
—1 Corinthians 11:29

notes

_____

_____

_____

_____

_____

_____

_____

New Life

Lesson Focus | On the Sunday after he was crucified, Jesus rose from the dead. He was again really and truly alive. He was not a ghost, but a man with a body that could eat and that his disciples could touch. He remained on earth for forty days, teaching his disciples all they needed to know to build his Church. Through his Resurrection, Christ proved that he is God, that he had redeemed us by his death, and that all who believe in him could also receive new life in him.

1 | begin

- Pray the Glory Be with your child.
- Ask your child to imagine that he was one of the Apostles. When he saw the risen Jesus, would he have believed it was Jesus? Why or why not? What would it have taken for him to believe?
- Read John 20:19–31 aloud.

2 | summarize

Summarize this week's lesson for your child:
Example: *When Jesus rose from the dead, he was truly living. He wasn't a ghost. In that, he showed us that all who love and follow him will receive the gift of eternal life too.*

3 | review

Review this week's lesson by asking your child the following questions:
1. How do we know the risen Jesus wasn't a ghost? (*The disciples could touch him, and he could eat.*)
2. What did Jesus' Resurrection prove? (*He was truly the Son of God, and that all he had said and done was true.*)
3. For how long did Jesus remain on earth after his Resurrection? (*Forty days.*)
4. What book of the Bible tells us what happened after Jesus' Ascension? (*The Acts of the Apostles.*)

References

- Student Textbook: Chapter 21, pp. 93–96
- Sacred Scripture: Mt 28:1–20; Luke 22:1–24:48; Jn 20:1–18; 21:2–18; Acts 1:1–12; 2:1–42, 9:1–22
- *Catechism of the Catholic Church*: 631–58, 727–30, 992–1004

4 | apply

Help your child apply this week's lesson by asking the following questions:

1. Although we will not have a glorified body until after we die, we have new life now through the gift of our Baptism. What does that new life help you to do?
2. Knowing you have Christ's life in you, how should you try to act at all times?
3. How can the Mass help you receive the gift of eternal life in heaven?

5 | conclude

- With your child, pray the Our Father.

6 | follow up

During the week, do at least one of the following activities with your child:

1. Memorize John 11:25.
2. Make a timeline of the events of Jesus' life, from the Annunciation through Saint Paul's conversion. Encourage your child to include as many events as he can from memory, then check it against the Gospel accounts.
3. Research and make a map of Saint Paul's missionary journeys after his conversion.

> *Jesus said to her, "I am the resurrection and the life; he who believes in me, though he die, yet shall he live."*
> —John 11:25

notes

_____

_____

_____

_____

_____

_____

_____

Come into the Lord's Presence Singing for Joy

Lesson Focus | The public worship of God by Catholics is called the Sacred Liturgy. As the Body of Christ, we honor God through our Liturgy, the Mass, partaking with the angels and saints in the worship of God that goes on in heaven. The Mass is divided into two main parts—the Liturgy of the Word and the Liturgy of the Eucharist—preceded by the Introductory Rites: an Entrance Antiphon or hymn, a greeting, the Penitential Rite, the Gloria, and the Collect (or Opening Prayer).

1 | begin

- Pray the Glory Be with your child.
- Ask your child how he would feel if a friend came over to your house for dinner, but when he walked into the house, he was dirty and refused to say hello, to speak to anyone, or to smile.
- Read Acts 2:42–46 aloud.

2 | summarize

Summarize this week's lesson for your child:

Example: *From the first days of the Church, Christians have gathered to worship God. By coming to Mass in our best clothes, paying attention, and participating from the very beginning in the Introductory Rites, we show God love, respect, and gratitude.*

3 | review

Review this week's lesson by asking your child the following questions:

1. What does the word liturgy mean? (*"Work of the people."*)
2. What is the basic structure of the Mass? (*Introductory Rites, Liturgy of the Word, Liturgy of the Eucharist, Concluding Rites.*)
3. What are the five parts of the Introductory Rites? (*Entrance Antiphon or hymn; greeting; Penitential Rite, Gloria, Opening Prayer or Collect.*)
4. What do Kyrie eleison and Christe eleison mean? (*"Lord have mercy" and "Christ have mercy."*)

References

- Student Textbook: Chapter 22, pp. 97–99
- Sacred Scripture: Jn 6:51; Acts 2:42, 46
- *Catechism of the Catholic Church*: 1105–6, 1163–73, 1345–55, 1362–66, 1383, 2842–45

4 | apply

Help your child apply this week's lesson by asking the following questions:
1. Why do you think it's important always to dress up for Mass? What does the way you're dressed say about how important you think Mass is?
2. Before Mass begins, how can you show respect for Jesus and the Sacred Liturgy?
3. During Mass, how can you show respect for Jesus, the Liturgy, and the congregation?

5 | conclude

- With your child, pray the Our Father.

6 | follow up

During the week, do at least one of the following activities with your child:
1. Memorize the first line in Latin for each of the major parts of the Mass (see Appendix).
2. Make a color wheel that displays each of the five liturgical colors, the Masses for which they're used, and the meaning of each color.
3. On Saturday night, have your child select his outfit for Mass the next day, and make sure it's clean and pressed.

notes

_____

_____

_____

_____

_____

_____

_____

Speak, Lord, Your Servant Is Listening

Lesson Focus | After the Introductory Rites, the Mass continues with the Liturgy of the Word. In the Introductory Rites, the congregation speaks to God. In the Liturgy of the Word, God speaks to the congregation. This happens through readings from the Old and New Testaments, as well as the homily. After the homily, the members of the congregation profess their faith, then present their petitions to God in the Prayers of the Faithful.

1 | begin

- Pray the Glory Be with your child.
- Tell your child about a book or story you've read more than once. Why did you read it multiple times? What different insights did you take away after each reading?
- Read Matthew 4:4 aloud.

2 | summarize

Summarize this week's lesson for your child:

Example: *God's Word, the Bible, is food for our spirits. There are always new insights to be gained and lessons learned from the Bible, for it is always God speaking to us, guiding us as we encounter new challenges and situations. That's why we read it at every Mass.*

3 | review

Review this week's lesson by asking your child the following questions:

1. What are the seven parts of the Liturgy of the Word? (*1. First Reading; 2. Responsorial Psalm; 3. Second Reading; 4. Gospel; 5. Homily; 6. Creed; 7. Prayers of the Faithful.*)
2. Is there a connection between the readings we hear at Mass? (*Yes, they are all related and selected to highlight a specific theme, which is often related to the day or season.*)
3. Can the readings at Mass come from any place other than the Bible? (*No.*)
4. What are the four Gospels? (*Matthew, Mark, Luke, and John.*)
5. Why do we sit during the readings and Responsorial Psalm. (*To show that we're listening and learning.*)
6. Why do we stand during the Gospel? (*To show our respect for Christ.*)

References

- Student Textbook: Chapter 23, pp. 100–102

- Sacred Scripture: 1 Sam 3:10; Mt 4:4; Lk 10:23–24; 1 Jn 4:6

- *Catechism of the Catholic Church*: 121–33, 185–97, 1345–55

4 | apply

Help your child apply this week's lesson by asking the following questions:
1. What is your favorite story from the Bible? What has it taught you?
2. Why do you think we need to profess what we believe in the Creed every Sunday? What temptations can lead us to forget, compromise, or be quiet about our beliefs?
3. Has God ever guided you or helped you through a reading from Scripture? How? How can you get more of the guidance you need from his Word?

5 | conclude

- With your child, pray the Our Father.

6 | follow up

During the week, do at least one of the following activities with your child:
1. Memorize Matthew 4:4.
2. On Saturday night, as a family, read the readings for the next day's Mass.
3. Write out your own Prayers of the Faithful. Have your child pray them aloud during family prayers.

But he answered, "It is written, 'Man shall not live by bread alone, but by every word that proceeds from the mouth of God.'"
—Matthew 4:4

notes

_____

_____

_____

_____

_____

_____

_____

Lift Up the Cup of Salvation

Lesson Focus | During the Liturgy of the Eucharist, bread and wine become the Body and Blood of Christ. This part of the Mass is rich with words and gestures that help us understand the offerings being made and the fruits those offerings will bear. It also contains prayers for the whole Church, as well as acts of adoration, thanks, and praise. It is the heart of our liturgical celebration, in which Christ offers himself to the Father and we, in turn, offer our lives to God.

1 | begin

- Pray the Glory Be with your child.
- Ask your child why people give gifts (e.g., as a sign of love, gratitude, and respect).
- Read Revelation 4:8 aloud.

2 | summarize

Summarize this week's lesson for your child:

Example: *In the Liturgy of the Eucharist, we give God gifts of praise, adoration, and thanksgiving. We also give ourselves. We give him these gifts for all the reasons people give gifts and also because it is right and just. God gives us a gift too: himself in the Eucharist.*

3 | review

Review this week's lesson by asking your child the following questions:

1. Of what does the Liturgy of the Eucharist consist? (*Offertory and Eucharistic Prayer.*)
2. What are the five parts of the Offertory? (*1. Preparation of the Altar; 2. Preparation of the Gifts; 3. Offering of the Gifts; 4. Washing of the Hands; 5. Prayers over the Gifts.*)
3. What should we offer to God during this part of the Mass? (*Our lives, sorrows, and joys.*)
4. How are we like the bread and wine? (*Just as the wheat is ground into flour for bread and grapes are crushed into wine, we must die to ourselves to become new and whole in Christ.*)
5. What are the seven parts of the Eucharistic Prayer? (*1. Preface; 2. Sanctus; 3. Prayer of Thanksgiving; 4. Invocation of the Holy Spirit; 5. Consecration; 6. Offering to the Father; 7. Doxology.*)
6. What happens during the Consecration? (*Transubstantiation—bread and wine become Christ's Body and Blood.*)

References

- Student Textbook: Chapter 24, pp. 103–106
- Sacred Scripture: Mt 21:9; Rev 4:8
- *Catechism of the Catholic Church*: 1061–65, 1333–36, 1345–55, 1373–88

4 | apply

Help your child apply this week's lesson by asking the following questions:

1. What things can you offer to God the next time you go to Mass?
2. Can you give me two examples of what it means to die to yourself?
3. How can you die to yourself every day? How can you die to yourself during the Mass?

5 | conclude

- With your child, pray the Our Father.

6 | follow up

During the week, do at least one of the following activities with your child:

1. Memorize Matthew 16:25.
2. Visit your parish's Adoration Chapel or tabernacle. Encourage your child to bring a prayer journal or sketchpad and write or draw the situations, trials, or gifts he can give to God.
3. Read about Saint Thérèse of Lisieux and her "Little Way."

For whoever would save his life will lose it, and whoever loses his life for my sake will find it.
—Matthew 16:25

notes

_____

_____

_____

_____

_____

_____

_____

Come to the Table of the Lord

Lesson Focus | The Communion Rite follows the Eucharistic Prayer. It is the celebration of the Eucharist as a sacred meal and the most intimate part of the Mass. At the invitation of the priest ("At the Savior's command and formed by divine teaching, we dare to say…") we pray the family prayer that Christ taught us (the Our Father). At the Last Supper, Jesus said "My peace I give you," and we express the sign of Christian friendship with one another in the Sign of Peace. We then acknowledge our unworthiness before the Lamb of God, receive Christ's Body and Blood into our body, and give thanks for that great gift.

1 | begin

- Pray the Glory Be with your child.
- Ask your child what he enjoys about family dinners. Why are they special?
- Read Matthew 6:9–13 aloud.

2 | summarize

Summarize this week's lesson for your child:

Example: *We say those same words at every Mass before receiving Communion. The Communion Rite is, in some ways, like a very special family meal. Receiving Christ brings us closer to him and to one another, strengthening us as individuals and as a family of believers.*

References

- Student Textbook: Chapter 25, pp. 107–10

- Sacred Scripture: Mt 5:23–24; 6:9–13; 8:5–13; Lk 17:12–19; Jn 14:27

- *Catechism of the Catholic Church*: 1333–1401, 2761–2856

3 | review

Review this week's lesson by asking your child the following questions:

1. Why is the Our Father such a perfect prayer? (*Because it contains all the petitions necessary for making us a holy, loving people of God.*)
2. What is the Rite of Peace? (*It is the time at Mass when the priest and people express peace and unity.*)
3. When you receive only the Sacred Host, do you receive less of Jesus than when you receive both the Host and from the chalice? (*No, all of Jesus, Body, Blood, Soul, and Divinity, is contained in every particle of the Host and in every drop of the Precious Blood.*)
4. What should we do after we receive Communion? (*Give thanks to God for the gift of himself and express our love and adoration of him in silent words of praise.*)

4 | apply

Help your child apply this week's lesson by asking the following questions:
1. Why do you think it's important never to receive Holy Communion unworthily?
2. How are all of us, in some way, unworthy to receive Christ?
3. For what can you thank God after Communion this Sunday?

5 | conclude

- With your child, pray the Our Father.

6 | follow up

During the week, do at least one of the following activities with your child:
1. Memorize John 14:27b.
2. After Mass, remain in church for a few minutes to thank God for his good gifts and the opportunity to worship him freely in public.

Let not your hearts be troubled, neither let them be afraid.
—John 14:27b

notes

_____

_____

_____

_____

_____

_____

_____

Preparing Our Hearts for Jesus

Lesson Focus | Long before we go to Mass, we should begin the work of preparing our hearts to receive Christ in Holy Communion. We do this through prayer, obeying God's commandments, being kind to others, learning more about our Faith, and following the example Jesus set at the Last Supper by serving others. When we fail to do this, we should go to God, who is waiting for us in confession.

1 | begin

- Pray the Glory Be with your child.
- Ask your child how he prepares for a sporting competition, recital, play, or test. Does he do well if he never practices or studies?
- Read Matthew 22:1–13 aloud.

2 | summarize

Summarize this week's lesson for your child:

Example: *The work of preparing our hearts to receive Jesus in Holy Communion begins long before we go to Mass. It's work we do every day and minute of our lives.*

3 | review

Review this week's lesson by asking your child the following questions:

1. What example did Jesus set for us at the Last Supper? (*He washed his disciples' feet, teaching us that we should seek to serve rather than be served.*)
2. Why was the guest at the wedding banquet in the parable turned away? (*Because he hadn't prepared himself as he should have.*)
3. What spiritual works can we do to prepare ourselves to receive Jesus? (*Pray, go to Adoration, go to confession, give to the Church, fast, sacrifice, etc.*)
4. What else can we do every day to prepare to receive Jesus? (*Be kind to others, give to the poor, never speak badly about anyone, avoid occasions of sin, help people in need, etc.*)
5. How can we grow in our love of Jesus and Holy Communion? (*Ask Jesus to help us love him more, obey his commandments, receive the Sacraments with greater devotion, study our Faith, etc.*)

References

- Student Textbook: Chapter 26, pp. 111–13

- Sacred Scripture: Mt 22:1–13; Jn 13:1–15

- *Catechism of the Catholic Church*: 468–69, 610–11, 1262–74, 1382–90, 1422–98

4 | apply

Help your child apply this week's lesson by asking the following questions:
1. What did you do this week to prepare your heart to receive Jesus?
2. What else could you have done to prepare your heart?
3. What are some obstacles that can prevent us from preparing our hearts as we should? How can we eliminate or get around those obstacles?

5 | conclude

- With your child, pray the Our Father.

6 | follow up

During the week, do at least one of the following activities with your child:
1. Memorize 1 Corinthians 9:24.
2. Write out the Anima Christi (see Appendix). Pray it as a family in the evenings, and pray it individually after Communion.
3. Pick one activity from your child's answer to question 2 in Step 4, and make a point to do that this week.

Do you not know that in a race all the runners compete, but only one receives the prize? So run that you may obtain it.
—1 Corinthians 9:24

notes

_____

_____

_____

_____

_____

_____

_____

Come, Lord Jesus

Lesson Focus | Jesus granted to his Apostles the power to bind and loose. One way the Apostles' successors—the Church's bishops—exercise that power is by setting the conditions under which the faithful may receive Holy Communion. Those conditions are that we must be in a state of grace (free from mortal sin), have fasted for one hour before receiving, and have a right intention (know whom we are about to receive and receive with appropriate reverence).

1 | begin

- Pray the Glory Be with your child.
- Remind your child of how you show respect for the valuables or furniture in your house (e.g., dirty shoes off inside, no feet on the sofa, no food in bedrooms, etc.).
- Read Matthew 16:13–20 aloud.

2 | summarize

Summarize this week's lesson for your child:

Example: *The Eucharist is far more precious than anything in our home. That's why the Church has used her authority to "bind and loose" to establish rules about how we are to receive the Eucharist. These rules help ensure that people treat the Eucharist with proper respect.*

References

- Student Textbook: Chapter 27, pp. 114–17
- Sacred Scripture: Is 22:20–25; Mt 16:13–20; Lk 10:16; Jn 21:1–29
- *Catechism of the Catholic Church*: 1355, 1373–90, 1524–25, 2041–43, 2120

3 | review

Review this week's lesson by asking your child the following questions:

1. What rules has the Church set to ensure proper respect for the Eucharist? (*We must be in a state of grace, have a right intention, and observe the Eucharistic fast.*)
2. What does it mean to be in a state of grace? (*To be free from mortal sin.*)
3. What is a right intention? (*We must be aware of the meaning of the Eucharist and act accordingly.*)
4. What is the Eucharistic fast? (*The obligation to take no food or drink except for water and medicine for one hour before receiving Holy Communion.*)
5. How often must Catholics receive the Eucharist? (*At least once a year during the Easter season.*)
6. What is Viaticum? (*Holy Communion for the dying. It means "provisions for the journey."*)

4 | apply

Help your child apply this week's lesson by asking the following questions:
1. How can you show respect for Jesus in Holy Communion during Mass?
2. How can you show respect for Jesus in Holy Communion when you receive?
3. How can you show respect for Jesus in Holy Communion after you've received?

5 | conclude

- With your child, pray the Our Father.

6 | follow up

During the week, do at least one of the following activities with your child:
1. Memorize 1 Corinthians 11:29.
2. Compose a prayer of thanksgiving for after Communion.
3. Learn about the Eucharistic miracle in Orvieto, Italy, and its connection to the feast of Corpus Christi.

For any one who eats and drinks without discerning the body eats and drinks judgment upon himself.
—1 Corinthians 11:29

notes

_____

_____

_____

_____

_____

_____

_____

_____

His Abiding Presence

Lesson Focus | Jesus remains with us always in the Blessed Sacrament, which is reserved in churches and chapels around the world. We can visit him there almost any time of the day and find comfort, strength, and guidance in his presence. We can also honor him through Benediction and Eucharistic processions and look upon him in Eucharistic Adoration. This perpetual presence is a great gift, and we should take advantage of it as often as possible.

1 | begin

- Pray the Glory Be with your child.
- Ask your child which he prefers: talking to you in person or talking to you through email or on the phone? Why? Tell him which you prefer and why.
- Together read John 14:13–21 aloud.

2 | summarize

Summarize this week's lesson for your child:

Example: *Jesus promised to be with us always, not just in thought, but truly with us. And he is. We can be with Jesus, in the same room with him—Body, Blood, Soul, and Divinity—every time we go to a Catholic church or chapel where the Blessed Sacrament is reserved.*

3 | review

Review this week's lesson by asking your child the following questions:

1. Where is the Eucharist reserved in a church? (*The tabernacle.*)
2. After Mass is over, is Christ still present in the Eucharist? (*Yes.*)
3. What do we call the object in which Jesus is placed in during Eucharistic Adoration? (*A monstrance.*)
4. What are some ways in which we can honor and be with the Eucharistic Jesus? (*Adoration, Benediction, Spiritual Communion, visits to the Blessed Sacrament, the Chaplet of the Blessed Sacrament, Eucharistic processions.*)
5. May some of the Precious Blood be reserved after Mass? (*No, it must all be consumed.*)
6. When the Host is broken, is Jesus broken? (*No, he is completely present in every particle.*)

References

- Student Textbook: Chapter 28, pp. 118–19
- Sacred Scripture: Jn 14:13–21
- *Catechism of the Catholic Church*: 464–70, 1113–17, 1378–90, 2691

4 | apply

Help your child apply this week's lesson by asking the following questions:

1. Why is it important to show reverence for Jesus when you pass a tabernacle or a place where the Eucharist is reserved? How can you do this?
2. What else can you do regularly to honor Jesus in the Eucharist?
3. How do you think time spent with Jesus in the Eucharist can help you love him and others more?

5 | conclude

- With your child, pray the Our Father.

6 | follow up

During the week, do at least one of the following activities with your child:

1. Memorize John 14:18.
2. As a family, go to Adoration and/or Benediction if a local parish offers it.
3. Learn about Saint Thomas Aquinas' devotion to the Eucharist and the poems and hymns he composed in honor of the Eucharistic Jesus. Or learn about how Saint Clare of Assisi turned back an army with the help of the Eucharistic Jesus.

> *I will not leave you desolate; I will come to you.*
> —John 14:18

notes

_____

_____

_____

_____

_____

_____

_____

Passage into Eternity

Lesson Focus | Just as the way we live our life every day helps prepare us for meeting Jesus in the Eucharist, so too does it prepare us for meeting Jesus at the hour of our death. As soon as we die, we will meet Jesus, and he will make known to us the measure of good and evil in us. The closer we are to him in this life and the more we strive to love him and others, the less we will fear that judgment and the more we will be filled with joy at the thought of being happy with him forever in heaven.

1 | begin

- Pray the Glory Be with your child.
- Show your child a picture of a loved one who has died. Tell him a favorite story about the person or describe his personality and the good he did while alive.
- Read Matthew 24:36–44 aloud.

2 | summarize

Summarize this week's lesson for your child:

Example: *Death can seem frightening, but really it's an opportunity to be happy forever in heaven with Jesus. The more we grow in love for him and do what he asks us to do now, the less frightening death will seem.*

3 | review

Review this week's lesson by asking your child the following questions:
1. What is death? (*The separation of body and soul.*)
2. What happens to the body at death? To the soul? (*The body returns to dust; the soul lives forever.*)
3. What will Jesus judge at the moment of our death? (*Our thoughts, words, deeds, and the good we failed to do.*)
4. What is this judgment called? (*The Particular Judgment.*)
5. Of what three things will we be immediately aware at the Particular Judgment? (*1. The exact balance of good and evil in our life; 2. the perfect justice of Jesus' judgment; 3. the presence of the Divine Judge, Jesus.*)

References

- Student Textbook: Chapter 29, pp. 123–25

- Sacred Scripture: Gen 2:4 — 3:24; Mt 22:1–14; 24:36–44; 25:1–13; Mk 13:30–37; Lk 12:35–40

- *Catechism of the Catholic Church*: 362–68, 1005–57, 1434–39, 1459–60, 2099–2100

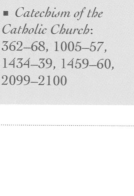

4 | apply

Help your child apply this week's lesson by asking the following questions:
1. Should we fear death? Why or why not?
2. What things can you do now to prepare to meet Jesus with a happy heart?
3. How do you think spending time with Jesus in the Eucharist now can help prepare you for the Particular Judgment?

5 | conclude

- With your child, pray the Our Father.

6 | follow up

During the week, do at least one of the following activities with your child:
1. Memorize John 5:24.
2. As a family, go to confession this week.
3. Visit the gravesite of a departed loved one, and say a prayer for him and the souls of others who are buried in the cemetery.

Truly, truly, I say to you, he who hears my word and believes him who sent me, has eternal life; he does not come into judgment, but has passed from death to life.
—John 5:24

notes

_____

_____

_____

_____

_____

_____

_____

Heaven—Purgatory—Hell

Lesson Focus | After this life, each of us will ultimately go to either heaven or hell. Heaven is a place of unimaginable happiness. The greatest happiness we can know in this life is only a dim shadow of the happiness souls in heaven know. Similarly, the greatest sorrow we can know in this life feels like nothing compared with the sorrow of the souls in hell. They are so sorrowful because they have cut themselves off from God, the source of all joy, by their own free will. Although some souls go straight to heaven, others must first pass through purgatory, where the last wounds of Original Sin are healed.

1 | begin

- Pray the Glory Be with your child.
- Ask your child to describe the most perfect day he has ever had or the most perfect day he can imagine.
- Together read John 14:1–4 aloud.

2 | summarize

Summarize this week's lesson for your child:

Example: *Because of Christ's death and Resurrection, if we open our hearts to receive all the grace he wants to give us in this life, we can spend an eternity of days that are all happier than the happiest day we can imagine.*

References

- Student Textbook: Chapter 30, pp. 126–29

- Sacred Scripture: Mt 5:22–26; 10:28–33; 25:41–46; Mk 9:42–48; Jn 14:1–4; 1 Cor 2:9; 1 Jn 3:2

- *Catechism of the Catholic Church*: 386–87, 1023–37, 1459–60, 1718–24, 1730–42

3 | review

Review this week's lesson by asking your child the following questions:

1. What do we call the angels and saints in heaven? (*The Church Triumphant.*)
2. What do we call the souls in purgatory? (*The Church Suffering.*)
3. What happens to souls in purgatory? (*They are purified of venial sin and the effects of sin.*)
4. What do the souls in purgatory think about? (*Their future union with God.*)
5. Who are the souls in hell? (*Those who have freely chosen to go there by rejecting God's mercy and love.*)
6. What is the greatest sorrow in hell? (*The absence of God.*)

4 | apply

Help your child apply this week's lesson by asking the following questions:
1. What choices can you make every day that will help you attain the happiness of heaven?
2. What can you do to help the souls in purgatory get to heaven sooner?
3. Why do you think anyone would choose hell? What could lead a person to make that choice?

5 | conclude

- With your child, pray the Our Father.

6 | follow up

During the week, do at least one of the following activities with your child:
1. Memorize Mark 8:36.
2. Have a Mass said at your parish for departed family members or a friend. Attend the Mass as a family.
3. In the afternoon or evening, pray the Divine Mercy Chaplet (see Appendix.)

For what does it profit a man, to gain the whole world and forfeit his life?
—Mark 8:36

notes

He Shall Come Again

Lesson Focus | One day, at the end of time, Jesus will come again to earth in great glory. Then every soul who has ever lived will participate in the General Judgment. The just and the unjust will be known to all; the bodies and souls of all will be reunited, with the just receiving a beautiful, glorified body; and Christ's righteousness and goodness will be made clear. His plan for each human soul, as well as his justice, will be shown to be perfect.

1 | begin

- Pray the Glory Be with your child.
- Search online for an image of Michelangelo's or Fra Angelico's painting of the Last Judgment. Have your child look at it carefully, then describe to you all that he sees.
- Read Mark 13:34–37 aloud.

2 | summarize

Summarize this week's lesson for your child:

Example: *At the end of time, Jesus will come again and his judgment on every single soul will be made known to all, as will the rightness and justness of his judgment.*

3 | review

Review this week's lesson by asking your child the following questions:
1. What is the Second Coming? (*The return of Jesus to earth at the end of time.*)
2. Will only the just be reunited with their bodies at the end of time? (*No, all will.*)
3. After the General Judgment, will purgatory still be needed? (*No.*)
4. At the General Judgment, what will everyone know about Jesus? (*That he is Lord and God and all his judgments are right and just.*)

References

- Student Textbook: Chapter 31, pp. 130–32

- Sacred Scripture: Mt 7:13–14; Mk 13:5–37; Lk 21:8–36; Acts 1:1–11; 2 Pet 3:10; Rev 21 — 22

- *Catechism of the Catholic Church*: 675–82, 988–1004, 1023–57, 2548–50

4 | apply

Help your child apply this week's lesson by asking the following questions:
1. How is the spiritual life like a race?
2. What will your resurrected body be able to do that your body can't do now?
3. Whose judgment should we care about more—God's or that of the people we know? Whose judgment do you care about more? How do you show this in your actions and thoughts?

5 | conclude

- With your child, pray the Our Father.

6 | follow up

During the week, do at least one of the following activities with your child:
1. Memorize 2 Timothy 4:7–8.
2. After school one day, visit your church to light a candle and say a prayer for a departed loved one.
3. Learn about Saint Joan of Arc, the injustice she faced, and the decisions she made. Encourage your child to dramatize her life with friends or siblings.

I have fought the good fight, I have finished the race, I have kept the faith. From now on there is laid up for me the crown of righteousness, which the Lord, the righteous judge, will award to me on that Day, and not only to me but also to all who have loved his appearing.
—2 Timothy 4:7–8

notes

_____
_____
_____
_____
_____
_____
_____
_____

The Life of Grace

Grade 7

*Let the earth bless the Lord;
let it sing praise to him and
highly exalt him for ever.*
Daniel 3:52

Lesson 1

Knowing God through Creation

Lesson Focus | Man knows God by both reason and faith. Reason tells us that he exists, that he has created a well-ordered world, and that he is powerful, beautiful, and knowable (to an extent) through his creation. Faith helps us believe what God has revealed about himself in Scripture and through the Incarnation—when God became man. We know he is a Blessed Trinity, all loving, all knowing, and present everywhere. Reason also helps us understand the things about God that we know by faith, while faith helps order our reason rightly.

1 | begin

- Pray the Glory Be with your child.
- Show your child a watch, cell phone, computer, or other household item with many working parts. Ask him if the item could have made itself. Does it have a designer? What can he know about the designer from the item? What can he not know?
- Read Matthew 16:13–20 aloud.

2 | summarize

Summarize this week's lesson for your child:

Example: *Just as we know this item has a maker, we know that the world, which is vastly more complex, must have a maker too. From looking at the world, we can know some things about its maker. We can know other things only by faith. Reason and faith together help us to know God.*

References

- Student Textbook: Chapter 1, pp. 13–17

- Sacred Scripture: Gen 1; Mt 16:13–20, 28:19; Acts 1:12–26, 15; 1 Tim 3:14–16; Heb 11

- *Catechism of the Catholic Church*: 27–28, 31–48, 153–65, 218–314, 688, 2810–12

3 | review

Review this week's lesson by asking your child the following questions:

1. How do we know God wants to be known? (*He reveals himself to us by faith and reason.*)
2. What does God reveal about himself in the Bible? (*That he is everywhere, knows everything, and is pure spirit; that he is love.*)
3. What does Jesus reveal to us about God? (*That he is a Holy Trinity.*)
4. Define the gift of faith. (*The supernatural power we receive from God that helps us believe in all he has revealed through the Bible, Jesus, and the Church.*)
5. How do humans image God? (*We have intelligence, understanding, and free will, as well as a spiritual and immortal soul.*)

4 | apply

Help your child apply this week's lesson by asking the following questions:
1. When you look at the world that God made, what does it tell you about him?
2. What is something that you know by faith to be true, and that your reason helps you understand?
3. How can you use your reason to understand your faith better?

5 | conclude

■ With your child, pray the Our Father.

6 | follow up

During the week, do at least one of the following activities with your child:
1. Memorize 2 Corinthians 5:7.
2. Hold a mock trial, in which your child must argue the case for God's existence using arguments grounded in both reason and faith.
3. Set aside five minutes every evening to read a short passage from the New Testament.

We walk by faith, not by sight.
—2 Corinthians 5:7

notes

_____

_____

_____

_____

_____

_____

_____

_____

Divine Revelation

Lesson Focus | God slowly revealed himself to men through the long centuries of human history, beginning with Adam and Eve, then continuing through the Jewish people. His fullest revelation of himself came through the person of Jesus Christ and what he revealed to his Apostles. Public revelation came to an end with the death of the last Apostle, John. It consists of Sacred Scripture (the Bible) and Sacred Tradition (God's Word handed on by Jesus to his Apostles and their successors). The Pope and the bishops are the guardians of both.

1 | begin

- Pray the Glory Be with your child.
- Have your family Bible on the table as you begin. Tell your child about a time when a passage or story from the Bible helped you, inspired you, or guided you.
- Read 2 Timothy 3:16–17 aloud.

2 | summarize

Summarize this week's lesson for your child:

Example: *The Bible speaks to us in every situation because it is God's Word, inspired by the Holy Spirit, and part of God's public revelation. We can trust that Sacred Scripture is God's Word because Sacred Tradition shows it to be so. Like faith and reason, the two work together.*

3 | review

Review this week's lesson by asking your child the following questions:

1. Why is the Bible free from error regarding religious truth? (*Because although men wrote it, the Holy Spirit inspired everything they wrote, protecting the writings from error.*)
2. Who is the primary author of Scripture? (*The Holy Spirit.*)
3. What are the two sections of the Bible? (*The Old Testament and the New Testament.*)
4. What types of books make up the Old Testament? (*The historical books, the wisdom books, and the prophetic books.*)
5. What types of books make up the New Testament? (*The Gospels, the Acts of the Apostles, Saint Paul's letters, letters to all Christians, the book of Revelation.*)
6. How do the Old and New Testaments work together? (*The Old Testament prepares us for the New, and the New helps us to understand the Old.*)

References

- Student Textbook: Chapter 2, pp. 18–23
- Sacred Scripture: Mt 26:17–30; Mk 14:13–26; Lk 22:8–39; 2 Tim 3:16–17
- *Catechism of the Catholic Church*: 50–95, 103–55, 185–97, 880–96

4 | apply

Help your child apply this week's lesson by asking the following questions:
1. What have you learned from the Bible that helps you understand the world better?
2. What have you learned from the Bible that has helped you love God and others better?
3. How has Sacred Tradition helped you to understand better what you've read in the Bible?

5 | conclude

- With your child, pray the Our Father.

6 | follow up

During the week, do at least one of the following activities with your child:
1. Memorize 2 Timothy 3:16–17.
2. Encourage your child to begin his private prayers by reading and meditating on a short passage from the Gospels.
3. Learn online about Hebrew and Greek, the languages in which the Bible was originally written. Find the alphabet for one and try learning the letters.

All Scripture is inspired by God and profitable for teaching, for reproof, for correction, and for training in righteousness, that the man of God may be complete, equipped for every good work.
—2 Timothy 3:16–17

notes

_____

_____

_____

_____

_____

_____

_____

Lesson 3

Creation

Lesson Focus | God is the Creator of heaven and earth. He made all things in existence out of nothing. The high point of creation was the human person, who uniquely images God through the powers of the intellect and the will. Although the first man and woman enjoyed perfect friendship with God and one another, they used their gift of free will to reject God's good plan and disobeyed him. For that sin—called Original Sin—they lost many of God's gifts and all their descendants inherited the wounds of their sin.

1 | begin

- Pray the Glory Be with your child.
- Tell your child about a particular virtue with which you struggle (e.g., being patient, not losing your temper, staying focused on your work, etc.).
- Read Genesis 3:1–8 aloud.

2 | summarize

Summarize this week's lesson for your child:

Example: *The world that God created was perfect, but because he wanted us to choose to love him, he gave us the gift of free will. Our first parents misused that gift, and all of creation suffered the consequences. That's what makes virtue difficult for us.*

3 | review

Review this week's lesson by asking your child the following questions:

1. Out of what did God create the world? (*Out of nothing.*)
2. What did God create? (*Material things, such as water and earth, and spiritual things, such as angels and human souls.*)
3. What are angels? (*Creatures who are pure spirit and are more intelligent and powerful than humans.*)
4. A human being is made up of what two things? (*A physical body and spiritual soul.*)
5. What are the effects of Original Sin on us? (*Separation from God, loss of grace, a tendency to sin, sickness, death.*)
6. What does the Redeemer of the human race do? (*Reconciles us to God and restores sanctifying grace to our souls.*)

References

- Student Textbook: Chapter 3, pp. 24–30
- Sacred Scripture: Gen 1–3; Rev 12:1–10
- Catechism of the Catholic Church: 280–412, 1023–37, 1730–48

4 | apply

Help your child apply this week's lesson by asking the following questions:

1. As a person, how are you different from animals? What can you do that animals can't do?
2. The gift to choose and do good comes with great responsibilities toward the rest of creation. How can you use those gifts in the world?
3. What virtue is the hardest for you to practice? What can strengthen that virtue in you?

5 | conclude

- With your child, pray the Our Father.

6 | follow up

During the week, do at least one of the following activities with your child:

1. Memorize Romans 5:19.
2. Before bed, pray the Prayer to Saint Michael Prayer (see Appendix).
3. Find online a recording of Joseph Haydn's oratorio *Creation* and listen to part or all of it. Ask your child to describe how it makes him feel. What does he imagine when he hears the music?

For as by one man's disobedience many were made sinners, so by one man's obedience many will be made righteous.
—Romans 5:19

notes

_____

_____

_____

_____

_____

_____

_____

_____

Lesson 4

God's Plan of Salvation

Lesson Focus | The story of how God prepared mankind for the coming of Jesus and how Jesus redeemed man and restored friendship with God is called salvation history. Unlike history books, which are written from a human perspective by human authors, salvation history is told by the Bible. It is history from God's perspective, and its primary author is the Holy Spirit. Major early figures in salvation history are Abraham, his son Isaac, his grandson Jacob/Israel, and his great-grandson Joseph.

1 | begin

- Pray the Glory Be with your child.
- Begin the lesson with both the Bible and your child's history textbook on the table. Ask what the books have in common. Then ask how they are different.
- Read Genesis 15 aloud.

2 | summarize

Summarize this week's lesson for your child:

Example: *The Bible is in many ways like a history book. It tells us the story of God's plan of salvation. Abraham is one of the key figures in that plan. Unlike your history book, however, it tells us history from God's perspective.*

3 | review

Review this week's lesson by asking your child the following questions:

1. Define salvation history. (*The events in history that tell the story of man's salvation.*)
2. What do we call the kind of agreement made between God and Israel? (*A covenant.*)
3. What is a patriarch, and who are the patriarchs in salvation history? (*A title given to the founding fathers of the Jewish people; Abraham, Isaac, Jacob, and Joseph.*)
4. What is a prefigurement? (*A person, place, or thing that comes before another person, place, or thing, is similar to what it comes before, and foretells it.*)
5. What did God promise Abraham? (*Many descendants who would become a great nation and live in the Promised Land.*)
6. How did Isaac prefigure Jesus? (*Abraham's near sacrifice of his beloved only son prefigured God the Father's sacrifice of Jesus, his only-begotten Son.*)

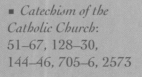

References

- Student Textbook: Chapter 4, pp. 31–34
- Sacred Scripture: Gen 12–22; 24–33; 35–37; 39–49
- *Catechism of the Catholic Church*: 51–67, 128–30, 144–46, 705–6, 2573

4 | apply

Help your child apply this week's lesson by asking the following questions:
1. What is your favorite story about the patriarchs? Why?
2. Can you relate to any of the experiences of the patriarchs? Which ones? Why?
3. How can knowing salvation history help you love God and others better?

5 | conclude

- With your child, pray the Our Father.

6 | follow up

During the week, do at least one of the following activities with your child:
1. Memorize Hebrews 12:1.
2. Have your child dramatize or illustrate one of his favorite scenes from Genesis.
3. Ask your child to write out four prayer petitions, one for each of the four patriarchs and each related to that patriarch's story (e.g., a petition asking Abraham for faith, Jacob for endurance, Joseph for trust. Include those petitions in family prayers this week.

> *Therefore, since we are surrounded by so great a cloud of witnesses, let us also lay aside every weight, and sin which clings so closely, and let us run with perseverance the race that is set before us.*
> —Hebrews 12:1

notes

_____

_____

_____

_____

_____

_____

_____

Lesson 5

The Holy Prophet Moses

Lesson Focus | Salvation history continues with Moses, who led God's people out of slavery in Egypt and toward the Promised Land. Through Moses, God gave the Israelites the Ten Commandments. When Moses died, Joshua led the Israelites into the Promised Land. For many years, Israel was ruled by representatives of God called judges, then God gave them a king. The first king of Israel was Saul; the second was David.

1 | begin

- Pray the Glory Be with your child.
- Find online a map of the Middle East in the ancient world. Have your child locate Egypt and Israel. Compare the map with a modern-day map.
- Read Exodus 3:7–12 aloud.

2 | summarize

Summarize this week's lesson for your child:

Example: *God continued salvation history with Moses, who led the Israelites out of Egypt; Joshua, who led them into the Promised Land; and David, Israel's great king.*

3 | review

Review this week's lesson by asking your child the following questions:

1. By what name did God reveal himself to Moses? (*Yahweh, which means "I AM."*)
2. What is the journey the Israelites took out of Egypt and into the Promised Land? (*The Exodus.*)
3. What two things did God require of Moses when he renewed his covenant with Israel? (*1. Obedience to the Ten Commandments; 2. Animal sacrifice.*)
4. What does consecrate mean? (*To set apart for God.*)
5. What is anointing? (*The pouring of oil on a person or thing as a sign of being chosen by God.*)
6. How did the Passover prefigure the Eucharist? (*The Israelites were saved from death and slavery when the lamb was sacrificed and eaten, and its blood was sprinkled on the doorpost. Jesus, the Lamb of God, was sacrificed, and his blood was shed to save us from slavery to sin and death. We eat the Lamb of God in the Eucharist.*)

References

- Student Textbook: Chapter 5, pp. 35–40
- Sacred Scripture: Ex 2–33; Lev 3–7; Josh 1, 6; Judg 16; 1 Sam 8–10, 16–17; 2 Sam 6–7
- *Catechism of the Catholic Church*: 62–64, 571, 1164, 1362–65, 2056–63, 2574–90

Mount Sinai.

4 | apply

Help your child apply this week's lesson by asking the following questions:
1. In what ways do you see yourself in the Israelites? What do you have in common with them?
2. What did you learn about God from his dealings with the Israelites?
3. Do you ever find yourself struggling to trust God or doubting his goodness? How can remembering the history of God and the Israelites help you through that struggle?

5 | conclude

- With your child, pray the Our Father.

6 | follow up

During the week, do at least one of the following activities with your child:
1. Memorize Psalm 117:2.
2. Walk through your church and find examples of persons and things that have been consecrated to God (e.g., saints who were religious, holy vessels, windows, etc.).
3. Pray an Act of Faith (see Appendix) during evening prayers.

> *For great is his mercy toward us; and the faithfulness of the LORD endures for ever. Praise the LORD!*
> —Psalm 117:2

notes

_____

_____

_____

_____

_____

_____

_____

Lesson 6

God's Special Spokesmen—The Prophets

Lesson Focus | To help prepare Israel for the coming Messiah, God sent many prophets to his people. The prophets' job was not so much to foretell the future as to give people a message from God about their present circumstances, a message to help them love God and others better. In Israel's history there are both major and minor prophets. Some of the most important prophets are Elijah, Elisha, Isaiah, and John the Baptist, the last prophet of the Old Testament.

1 | begin

- Pray the Glory Be with your child.
- Tell your child about a time you had to correct a friend or loved one who was doing something wrong and harmful to his soul. How did that person react?
- Read Matthew 3:1–12 aloud.

2 | summarize

Summarize this week's lesson for your child:

Example: *John the Baptist was the last and greatest prophet of Israel. He was also Jesus' cousin. Like all prophets, John was often unpopular because he called people to give up their sin and repent. Also, like all prophets, he helped prepare people for Jesus, the Messiah.*

3 | review

Review this week's lesson by asking your child the following questions:
1. Define prophet. (*A person chosen by God to be his messenger to his people.*)
2. What do we call the messages God gave through his prophets? (*Prophecies.*)
3. What does Messiah mean? (*"Anointed One."*)
4. Who are the four major prophets? (*Isaiah, Jeremiah, Daniel, and Ezekiel.*)
5. Who are the twelve minor prophets? (*Hosea, Joel, Amos, Obadiah, Jonah, Micah, Nahum, Habakkuk, Zephaniah, Haggai, Zechariah, and Malachi.*)
6. Who are Elijah and Elisha? (*Important early prophets who left no writings behind.*)

References

- Student Textbook: Chapter 6, pp. 41–44
- Sacred Scripture: 1 Kings 18; 2 Kings 1–2; 4; Is 52:13—53:12; Mt 3
- *Catechism of the Catholic Church*: 64, 436, 523–24, 717–20

4 | apply

Help your child apply this week's lesson by asking the following questions:

1. Why do you think the prophets were so unpopular? Do you think it was easy or hard for them to be God's messengers? Why?
2. Why is it so hard to repent for what we've done wrong? Why don't we like it when people correct our wrong actions?
3. What do you think a prophet of God would have to say to our world today?

5 | conclude

- With your child, pray the Our Father.

6 | follow up

During the week, do at least one of the following activities with your child:

1. Memorize Acts 10:43.
2. Have your child call a grandparent or godparent to explain what the prophets told Israel.
3. As a family, pray the Divine Mercy Chaplet (see Appendix.)

> *To him all the prophets bear witness that every one who believes in him receives forgiveness of sins through his name.*
> —Acts 10:43

notes

_____
_____
_____
_____
_____
_____
_____

Lesson 7

Our Lord and Savior Jesus Christ

Lesson Focus | After many centuries of waiting, Jesus, the promised Messiah, came into the world. Just as the prophets had foretold, he was born of a virgin in Bethlehem under a great shining star. He was raised in a human family and was like us in all things but sin. At the same time, Jesus was divine. He had two natures—one divine and one human—united in one Divine Person. Through the centuries, many heresies have denied his divinity or his humanity, but the Church has defended the truth about Christ.

1 | begin

- Pray the Glory Be with your child.
- Find an image of Jesus in your house and look at it with your child. Ask him to describe what he sees. Does Jesus look different from other people?
- Read Mark 4:35–41 aloud.

2 | summarize

Summarize this week's lesson for your child:

Example: *At first glance, Jesus looked ordinary. But no ordinary person could stop a storm. Only God could do that. That's who Jesus, the promised Messiah, was—fully God and fully man.*

3 | review

Review this week's lesson by asking your child the following questions:
1. Who is called the Immaculate Conception? Why? (*Mary; she was conceived without sin.*)
2. What term describes Jesus' taking on our human nature and becoming man? (*The Incarnation.*)
3. What heresy taught that Jesus was not human? (*Docetism.*)
4. What heresy taught that Jesus was not God? (*Arianism.*)
5. What do we call the writers of the Gospels? (*Evangelists.*)
6. Was Jesus ever tempted to sin? Did he sin? (*Yes; no.*)
7. By whose power did Jesus work miracles? (*His own.*)

References

- Student Textbook: Chapter 7, pp. 47–51

- Sacred Scripture: Mt 3; Mk 4:35–41; Lk 1:28–38; 4:33–37; 7:13; Jn 2:1–11; 11:5, 35

- *Catechism of the Catholic Church*: 422–540, 871–96

4 | apply

Help your child apply this week's lesson by asking the following questions:
1. If you had been alive during Jesus' time on earth, which of his miracles would have convinced you he was God? Why?
2. What wrong beliefs about Jesus have you encountered? How can you help correct those wrong beliefs when you encounter them?
3. What experiences or emotions do you and Jesus have in common? How does it make you feel about God to know that he has felt and done some of the same things as you?

5 | conclude

- With your child, pray the Our Father.

6 | follow up

During the week, do at least one of the following activities with your child:
1. Memorize John 1:14a.
2. As a family, say the Prayer to the Sacred Heart of Jesus (see Appendix). If you don't have an image of the Sacred Heart in your house, consider buying one as a reminder of Jesus' great love.
3. Learn about Saint Margaret Mary Alacoque and the devotion to the Sacred Heart.

> *And the Word became flesh and dwelt among us, full of grace and truth.*
> —John 1:14a

notes

_____

_____

_____

_____

_____

_____

_____

The Saving Mission of Jesus

Lesson Focus | God the Father sent his only-begotten Son into the world to redeem us from sin. Jesus did that by dying on the Cross. God also sent Jesus as a prophet, to teach us how to live in the way most pleasing to him. Likewise, Jesus is our one high priest, who offered himself on the Cross as a sacrifice in atonement for our sins. Now Jesus reigns as King in the Kingdom of God. As part of the Mystical Body of Christ, all Christians share Christ's call to be priests, prophets, and kings.

1 | begin

- Pray the Glory Be with your child.
- Show your child a picture of his Baptism. Ask him if he knows what spiritual gifts he received that day.
- Read Matthew 13:44–46 aloud.

2 | summarize

Summarize this week's lesson for your child:

Example: *God sent Jesus into this world to redeem us. He came as a priest, prophet, and king. Each of us, at our Baptism and Confirmation, receives the grace also to be a priest, prophet, and king.*

3 | review

Review this week's lesson by asking your child the following questions:

1. How did Jesus show his love for the Father? (*By doing the will of God.*)
2. What is the Good News? (*God loves us, and Jesus came to take away our sins.*)
3. How is Jesus a prophet? (*He told us the Good News and how to please God.*)
4. How is Jesus a priest? (*He offered himself on the Cross as a sacrifice for our sins.*)
5. Over what kingdom does Jesus reign? (*The Kingdom of God.*)
6. What are parables? (*Stories Jesus told about the Kingdom of God.*)

References

- Student Textbook: Chapter 8, pp. 52–54
- Sacred Scripture: Mt 5:1–12; 11:1; 13:44–46; 16:18–19; 25:31–46; Jn 14:26
- *Catechism of the Catholic Church*: 422–546, 783–86, 901–13, 2746–51

4 | apply

Help your child apply this week's lesson by asking the following questions:

1. As a prophet, Jesus shared the Good News. How does God call you to be a prophet in the world today?
2. As a priest, Jesus offered the sacrifice of himself. What kind of sacrifices does God expect you, as part of his priestly people, to offer every day?
3. As King, Jesus reigns in the Kingdom of God. We're all called to reign over ourselves, being the master of our words and deeds. How can you do this every day?

5 | conclude

- With your child, pray the Our Father.

6 | follow up

During the week, do at least one of the following activities with your child:

1. Memorize John 3:16.
2. On Friday, make a small sacrifice to help someone you know who is in need.
3. As a family, pray the third Luminous Mystery: The Proclamation of the Kingdom of God.

> *For God so loved the world that he gave his only-begotten Son, that whoever believes in him should not perish but have eternal life.*
> —John 3:16

notes

_____

_____

_____

_____

_____

_____

_____

Lesson 9

The Priesthood of Jesus

Lesson Focus | Ever since the Fall, men have offered sacrifices to God as a way of atoning for their sins, worshipping him, and giving thanks. All these sacrifices had three things in common: a priest, a victim, and an altar. None of these sacrifices, however, could truly atone for sin. Jesus' sacrifice on the Cross, however, changed that. He offered the perfect sacrifice, as both perfect priest and spotless victim, on the Cross. He is also our priestly mediator, interceding for us in heaven and restoring friendship between God and man.

1 | begin

- Pray the Glory Be with your child.
- Show your child a crucifix. Ask him to describe what he sees.
- Read Hebrews 7:23—8:6 aloud.

2 | summarize

Summarize this week's lesson for your child:

Example: *Every time we see a crucifix, we should see Christ as our perfect high priest, offering himself as a spotless victim in sacrifice on the altar of the Cross. We should also see God's love and Christ restoring the bonds of friendship between God and man with his perfect mediation.*

3 | review

Review this week's lesson by asking your child the following questions:

1. What is a priest? (*Someone chosen to pray and offer sacrifice to God on behalf of others.*)
2. What must the victim in a sacrifice be? (*A living being offered to God.*)
3. What is an altar? (*Where a sacrifice takes place.*)
4. What three things do we learn about sacrifice from the Old Testament? (*1. The gift must be offered with a pure and sinless heart; 2. The offering is a thanksgiving to God for his blessing and protection; 3. Sacrifice shows sorrow for sin and a desire for forgiveness.*)
5. Who was Melchizedek? (*The priest–king of Salem [Jerusalem], who offered bread and wine to God, just as Jesus offered bread and wine to the Father at the Last Supper.*)
6. What did Jesus' sacrifice do that the sacrifices of the Old Testament could not do? (*Made up for every sin and reconciled us to the Father.*)

References

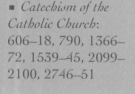

- Student Textbook: Chapter 9, pp. 55–58
- Sacred Scripture: Gen 4:1–8; 14:17–24; Heb 7:1–10; 7:23—8:6; 10:11–23
- *Catechism of the Catholic Church*: 606–18, 790, 1366–72, 1539–45, 2099–2100, 2746–51

4 | apply

Help your child apply this week's lesson by asking the following questions:

1. What are some examples of sacrifices you've made?
2. What are some things that prevent our sacrifices from being perfect? What wrong intentions might we sometimes have when we offer a sacrifice?
3. How can we work to purify our intentions when we make sacrifices?

5 | conclude

- With your child, pray the Our Father.

6 | follow up

During the week, do at least one of the following activities with your child:

1. Memorize Hebrews 5:1.
2. Learn about Saint Thérèse's "Little Way." As a family, talk about different ways you can start living the Little Way.
3. Learn online how to make a Saint Thérèse chaplet out of beads and string. Once the chaplet is made, begin saying it on Fridays.

> *For every high priest chosen from among men is appointed to act on behalf of men in relation to God, to offer gifts and sacrifices for sins.*
> —Hebrews 5:1

notes

_____

_____

_____

_____

_____

_____

_____

Christ, Source of All Grace

Lesson Focus | God never asks anyone to do the impossible. He always gives us the grace we need to carry out the mission entrusted to us. Jesus is the perfect example of this. He was perfectly equipped to redeem us from our sin and proclaim the Good News. In dying on the Cross, he won for us the grace of redemption, which means that whoever believes in him can have new life. We receive this grace in Baptism and through the other Sacraments. The source of the grace, however, is Christ himself.

1 | begin

- Pray the Glory Be with your child.
- Turn on the water at your kitchen sink. Ask your child where the water comes from.
- Read Matthew 28:19 aloud.

2 | summarize

Summarize this week's lesson for your child:

Example: *Just as the faucet is the means by which water comes to us, not the actual source of the water, so too are Baptism and the other Sacraments the means by which grace comes to us, while Christ is the actual source of all grace.*

3 | review

Review this week's lesson by asking your child the following questions:

1. What does it mean to redeem someone? (*To buy someone's freedom from slavery.*)
2. Through whom does Jesus give the grace of God to all who believe? (*Priests.*)
3. By which Sacrament do we receive the grace of new life? (*Baptism.*)
4. How was our new life made possible? (*By Jesus' suffering, death, and Resurrection.*)
5. What does grace do for us? (*It makes us children of God and allows us to go to heaven.*)
6. Define mediatrix. (*A title for Mary. It reminds us that Jesus came to us through her and now she prays for us in heaven.*)

References

- Student Textbook: Chapter 10, pp. 59–62

- Sacred Scripture: Mt 9:1–8; 16:13–20; 28:19; Mk 1:23–28; 2:2–12

- *Catechism of the Catholic Church*: 35, 547, 968–70, 1127–29, 1987–2011

4 | apply

Help your child apply this week's lesson by asking the following questions:

1. Besides receiving the Sacraments, what are some things you can do to grow in grace?
2. What things can you do every day that can weaken the life of grace in you?
3. In what situations do you turn to Mary for help? At what other times could you turn to her?

5 | conclude

- With your child, pray the Our Father.

6 | follow up

During the week, do at least one of the following activities with your child:

1. Memorize John 1:16.
2. Learn the Memorare (see Appendix). Develop the habit of praying it with your child when you hear an ambulance or a fire siren or when you or someone else is in great need.
3. Write a story about or draw a picture of one of the people Jesus healed. Depict his life both before and after the miracle. Imagine how his life and personality changed, and try to convey that in the story or picture.

> *And from his fullness have we all received, grace upon grace.*
> —John 1:16

notes

_____

_____

_____

_____

_____

_____

_____

Lesson 11

Jesus Founds His Church

Lesson Focus | For thousands of years, God's chosen people were related by blood. They were the Israelites. When Christ came, however, all who believed in him became part of his new chosen people, the Church. Christ founded the Church to continue his saving work on earth. He established a hierarchy, beginning with the Apostles, to govern his Church and administer the Sacraments. We know that the Catholic Church is the Church founded by Christ because it bears the four identifying marks: it is one, holy, catholic, and apostolic.

1 | begin

- Pray the Glory Be with your child.
- Search online for pictures of Saint Peter's Basilica in Rome and show them to your child. Look at images of both the inside and the outside.
- Read Matthew 16:16–19 aloud.

2 | summarize

Summarize this week's lesson for your child:

Example: *During his time on earth, Jesus established his Church. The Church is the new chosen people of God, Christ's Mystical Body on earth. Christ continues his work through her. She is guided by the Pope, Peter's successor in Rome, and the bishops, the Apostles' successors.*

3 | review

References

- Student Textbook: Chapter 11, pp. 63–68

- *Sacred Scripture:* Is 22:22–23; Mt 16:16–19; Mk 1:16–20; Lk 5:24–28; Jn 1:35–51

- *Catechism of the Catholic Church:* 760, 128–29, 851–913

Review this week's lesson by asking your child the following questions:

1. What are the four marks of the Church? (*One, holy, catholic, and apostolic.*)
2. In what three places can the Church be found? (*Heaven, purgatory, and earth.*)
3. What do we call the Church in those three places? (*The Church Triumphant, the Church Suffering, and the Church Militant.*)
4. Name the twelve Apostles. (*Simon Peter; James, son of Zebedee; John, brother of James; Andrew; Philip; Bartholomew; Matthew; Thomas; James, son of Alphaeus; Jude Thaddeus; Simon the Cananaean; and Judas Iscariot.*)
5. How is the Church a pilgrim Church? (*We are all on a spiritual journey to heaven.*)
6. How is the Church a Mystical Body? (*Christ is the head and her members are the different parts, each with different jobs and different gifts, and each directed by Christ.*)

4 | apply

Help your child apply this week's lesson by asking the following questions:

1. How does it feel to know you have friends in heaven and purgatory praying for you and wanting to help you all the time? How often do you ask for their help?
2. What are some things you can do to help those who are part of the Church Suffering?
3. What gifts did God give you to help the members of his Body? How can you use those gifts in the future?

5 | conclude

- With your child, pray the Our Father.

6 | follow up

During the week, do at least one of the following activities with your child:

1. Memorize 1 Corinthians 14:12.
2. Research your bishop: where he grew up, where he went to school, why he became a priest, etc.
3. Find online a novena to your child's patron or favorite saint. As a family, pray the novena for nine days for a special intention.

> *So with yourselves; since you are eager for manifestations of the Spirit, strive to excel in building up the Church.*
> —1 Corinthians 14:12

notes

_____

_____

_____

_____

_____

_____

_____

The Church in Our Time

Lesson Focus | After Jesus' Ascension, the Holy Spirit came to the Apostles, giving them the courage and strength to preach the gospel all over the world. Through the centuries, the Holy Spirit has protected the Church with the gifts of infallibility and indefectibility. To make the Good News understandable to all people in all times, the Church can change some of her rules about worship, but never her message, doctrines, or moral law.

1 | begin

- Pray the Glory Be with your child.
- Show your child a picture of the Pope. If you've ever seen him in person, tell your child about that experience.
- Read Acts 2:1–4 aloud.

2 | summarize

Summarize this week's lesson for your child:

Example: *Because of the Holy Spirit, the Church will endure on earth until the end of time. Some of her rules, called disciplines, may change, but her teachings and mission never will.*

3 | review

Review this week's lesson by asking your child the following questions:

1. Define *infallibility*. (*The special protection given by the Holy Spirit to the Pope, and all the bishops when they teach in union with the Pope, that prevents the Catholic Church from teaching error in matters of faith and morals.*)
2. Define *indefectibility*. (*The truth that the Catholic Church will endure on earth until the end of time. Nothing will be able to destroy her.*)
3. Define *martyrdom*. (*Dying for the sake of the Gospel.*)
4. Define *missionary*. (*One who tells others about the Faith.*)
5. What is a rite? (*A way of celebrating the Sacraments—especially the Mass—the Liturgy of the Hours, and blessings.*)

References

- Student Textbook: Chapter 12, pp. 69–72
- Sacred Scripture: Acts 2:1–4; 6:1–8
- *Catechism of the Catholic Church*: 731–41, 763–80, 814, 830, 849–59, 888–92, 1200–9

4 | apply

Help your child apply this week's lesson by asking the following questions:

1. Why do you think the Holy Spirit gives the Church the gift of infallibility?
2. How can you be a missionary right now, in your everyday life?
3. Through the centuries, many Catholics have faced great persecution for their beliefs. For what things are Catholics in our culture persecuted? Have you ever been persecuted by anyone for any of those reasons? Do you think you ever will be?

5 | conclude

- With your child, pray the Our Father.

6 | follow up

During the week, do at least one of the following activities with your child:

1. Memorize Matthew 16:18.
2. On Sunday, attend a Catholic Church where Mass is celebrated in a different rite or form of rite (e.g., Byzantine, Maronite, Anglican Use Roman Rite, Extraordinary Form Roman Rite, etc.). Before you go, learn more about the rite online.
3. Make a map of all the places the Apostles went after Jesus died. Mark the places where each of the Apostles was martyred and how he died.

And I tell you, you are Peter, and on this rock I will build my Church, and the gates of Hades shall not prevail against it.
—Matthew 16:18

notes

_____

_____

_____

_____

_____

_____

_____

Lesson 13

Doctrine of Grace

Lesson Focus | Grace is God's free gift to us. We cannot merit it. God gives it to us simply because he loves us. There are two types of grace: sanctifying and actual. Sanctifying grace is God's life in our souls. It gives us the theological virtues of faith, hope, and charity, comes to us in Baptism and the other Sacraments, and can be lost only through mortal sin. Actual grace comes to us in the form of inspirations to do good things. When we say yes to those inspirations, we grow in virtue. Actual graces help make the Christian life possible.

1 | begin

- Pray the Glory Be with your child.
- Tell your child about a time you had to do something that required great virtue. Explain that you could not have made that choice without the help of grace.
- Read 1 John 3:15–24 aloud.

2 | summarize

Summarize this week's lesson for your child:

Example: *All the good things we're able to do, think, and believe are the result of God's grace working in our life. He gives us sanctifying grace, his life, through the Sacraments, and actual graces every moment of the day. Our job is to say yes to the grace he offers.*

3 | review

Review this week's lesson by asking your child the following questions:
1. Define *grace*. (*The free gift God gives us by which he helps us reach heaven.*)
2. Define *supernatural*. (*Possible only for God; above the powers of man or nature.*)
3. What does sanctifying grace do for us? (*It gives us a share in God's own life, making us his adopted children and making it possible for us to be with him in heaven.*)
4. What is actual grace? (*Day-to-day helps that enlighten our mind and strengthen our will so that we may do good and avoid evil.*)
5. What are some examples of actual graces? (*The desire to pray, to read the Bible, to help a person in need, etc.*)
6. How does grace help us attain our purpose on earth? (*Receiving grace and acting in accord with it enables us to know, love, and serve God so we can be with him in heaven.*)
7. Who were the two people born after the Fall with sanctifying grace? (*Jesus and Mary.*)

References

- Student Textbook: Chapter 13, pp. 75–77
- Sacred Scripture: Jn 1:12, 18; 3:5; 1 Pet 1:23; 2 Pet 1:4; 1 Jn 3
- *Catechism of the Catholic Church*: 35, 683, 1127–29, 1250, 1996–2011

4 | apply

Help your child apply this week's lesson by asking the following questions:
1. What are some things sanctifying grace helps you believe, trust, or love?
2. Tell me about a time you said yes when God offered you actual graces to do something good. Tell me about a time you said no.
3. How can you thank God for the graces he gives you in the Sacraments and every day?

5 | conclude

- With your child, pray the Our Father.

6 | follow up

During the week, do at least one of the following activities with your child:
1. Memorize Romans 8:11.
2. As a family, go to Mass on at least one extra day besides Sunday.
3. Pray the Prayer to My Guardian Angel (see Appendix) every morning, and encourage your child to ask his guardian angel for help in saying yes to the actual graces God will offer him that day.

If the Spirit of him who raised Jesus from the dead dwells in you, he who raised Christ Jesus from the dead will give life to your mortal bodies also through his Spirit who dwells in you.
—Romans 8:11

notes

Faith, Hope, and Charity

Lesson Focus | At our Baptism, God gave us three supernatural powers, powers that would not be possible without his help. These powers are called the theological virtues: faith, hope, and charity. Faith is the power to believe in God and what the Church teaches. Hope is the power to trust in God and his promises. Charity is the ability to love God and our neighbor. As long as we are not in a state of mortal sin, we have these powers. We can strengthen them through good works and prayer.

1 | begin

- Pray the Glory Be with your child.
- Look at the drawings on this page. Ask your child to identify each symbol and explain why that symbol was chosen to represent the virtue.
- Read 1 Corinthians 13 aloud.

2 | summarize

Summarize this week's lesson for your child:

Example: *As long as we are in a state of sanctifying grace, we have the power to believe, trust, and love. These powers are the theological virtues: faith, hope, and charity.*

3 | review

Review this week's lesson by asking your child the following questions:
1. What is the difference between natural and supernatural virtues? (*Natural virtues are attained by repeating good acts. Supernatural virtues are given directly by God.*)
2. What is a theological virtue? (*A virtue that comes from God and helps us live for him.*)
3. Define *faith*. (*The theological virtue by which we believe God and all that he has revealed through the Church.*)
4. Define *hope*. (*The theological virtue by which we trust in and rely on God.*)
5. Define *charity*. (*The theological virtue by which we love God above all things for his own sake and love our neighbors as ourselves.*)
6. What does it mean to love God? To love others? (*Loving God is wanting to please him; loving others is wanting what's best for them.*)

References

- Student Textbook: Chapter 14, pp. 78–81

- Sacred Scripture: Jn 13:1, Rom 1:17; 1 Cor 13:1–7, 13; Gal 5:6; Heb 6:19–20; 10:23; 2 Pet 1:4

- *Catechism of the Catholic Church*: 1803–29, 2095–96, 2656–58

4 | apply

Help your child apply this week's lesson by asking the following questions:
1. Can you give me two examples of what faith helps you to do?
2. Can you give me two examples of how hope helps you?
3. Can you give me two examples of actions motivated by charity?

5 | conclude

- With your child, pray the Our Father.

6 | follow up

During the week, do at least one of the following activities with your child:
1. Memorize 1 Corinthians 13:3.
2. Watch one of your child's favorite television shows together. Afterward, talk with him about how human love is depicted. Is the love charity—wanting another's best? Or is it more of a selfish feeling?
3. Each day, pray one of the following prayers from the Appendix: an Act of Faith, an Act of Hope, or an Act of Charity.

If I give away all I have, and if I deliver my body to be burned, but have not love, I gain nothing.
—1 Corinthians 13:3

notes

_____

_____

_____

_____

_____

_____

_____

Lesson 15

The Cardinal Virtues

Lesson Focus | God calls all his children to live good lives. That's how we show him our love for him. Whether we live a good life depends on how well we practice virtue and avoid vice. Virtues are good habits. Vices are bad habits. There are four cardinal virtues on which our ability to practice other virtues depends: prudence, justice, temperance, and fortitude.

1 | begin

- Pray the Glory Be with your child.
- Ask your child to tell you how he became good at something, such as a sport, a subject in school, or a game. Did he become better at that activity the more he practiced it?
- Read Matthew 5:1–11 aloud.

2 | summarize

Summarize this week's lesson for your child:

Example: *If we want to become good at living as Christ wants us to live, we have to practice the virtues, starting with the cardinal virtues, those on which all other virtues depend: prudence, justice, temperance, and fortitude.*

3 | review

Review this week's lesson by asking your child the following questions:
1. Define *prudence*. (*The virtue that helps us make right decisions, judge what is good, and choose the right means of attaining it.*)
2. Define *justice*. (*The virtue that helps us respect the rights of others and give others what is due to them.*)
3. Define *temperance*. (*The power to control and direct ourselves and our desires.*)
4. Define *fortitude*. (*The power to face difficulty and danger in the pursuit of good with peace and courage.*)
5. What are the seven capital sins or principal vices? (*Pride, avarice, lust, anger, gluttony, envy, sloth.*)
6. How do we overcome those sins? (*By practicing their opposite virtues: humility, liberality, chastity, patience, sobriety, brotherliness, diligence in the service of God.*)

References

- Student Textbook: Chapter 15, pp. 82–86

- Sacred Scripture: Mt 5:1–11

- *Catechism of the Catholic Church*: 1716–29, 1763–70, 1804–11, 1866

4 | apply

Help your child apply this week's lesson by asking the following questions:

1. Can you give me an example of what it means to exercise the virtue of prudence? Temperance? Justice? Fortitude?
2. What is an example of pride? Avarice? Lust? Anger? Gluttony? Envy? Sloth?
3. What is an example of humility? Liberality? Chastity? Patience? Sobriety? Brotherliness? Diligence in the service to God?

5 | conclude

- With your child, pray the Our Father.

6 | follow up

During the week, do at least one of the following activities with your child:

1. Memorize 2 Peter 1:5.
2. Talk to your child about which of the seven capital sins he struggles with the most. Together, come up with a list of things he can do to practice that vice's opposite virtue.
3. Learn more about Saint Dominic Savio and how he avoided mortal sin through self-discipline. Encourage your child to pray to him for help in practicing the same virtue and look for specific ways in his daily routine to imitate him (e.g., getting up promptly every day.)

> *For this very reason make every effort to supplement your faith with virtue, and virtue with knowledge.*
> —2 Peter 1:5

notes

_____

_____

_____

_____

_____

_____

_____

Lesson 16

The Seven Sacraments

Lesson Focus | On the Cross, Christ won sanctifying grace for men. To give that grace to us, he instituted the seven Sacraments. Those Sacraments are efficacious signs: they not only represent spiritual realities, but they also make those realities possible. Each Sacrament also confers a special grace, unique to it. This is called a Sacramental grace.

1 | begin

- Pray the Glory Be with your child.
- Together, look at pictures taken on the days your child first received all the Sacraments he has celebrated thus far.
- Read Matthew 28:18–20 aloud.

2 | summarize

Summarize this week's lesson for your child:

Example: *The seven Sacraments are the means by which we receive sanctifying grace, and they impart specific sacramental graces to help us in the Christian life. Baptism is the first Sacrament we receive.*

3 | review

Review this week's lesson by asking your child the following questions:
1. What is a Sacrament? (*A sign instituted by Christ to give us grace.*)
2. What is a sign? (*A word or symbol that gives us a message.*)
3. What is an efficacious sign? (*A sign that causes what it signifies. It makes it happen.*)
4. Does the Sacrament's power depend on the holiness of the minister? (*No.*)
5. What is the specific sacramental grace imparted by the seven Sacraments? (*1. Baptism—the grace to live a holy life; 2. Confirmation—the grace to be strong in faith; 3. Eucharist—the grace to love Jesus and our neighbors; 4. Penance—the grace to overcome sin; 5. Anointing—healing in body or soul, or both, and the grace to accept suffering and death; 6. Holy Orders—the grace for priests to live out their vocation; 7. Matrimony—grace for the couple to love one another and be good parents.*)

References

- Student Textbook: Chapter 16, pp. 87–91

- Sacred Scripture: Mt 19:6; 28:18–19; Jn 20:19–23; Acts 6:1–7; 8:14–17; 1 Cor 11:24–26; Jas 5:14

- *Catechism of the Catholic Church*: 738–40, 950, 1077–1189

4 | apply

Help your child apply this week's lesson by asking the following questions:

1. For each of the Sacraments you have received, tell me one way the grace of that Sacrament has helped you to be a better, more virtuous, and loving person.
2. How do you think going to confession frequently could help you overcome sin? How? Do you think you go to confession as often as you should? Why or why not?
3. How do you think going to Mass more than once a week could help you love Jesus and others more? Do you think you go to Mass as often as you should? Why or why not?

5 | conclude

- With your child, pray the Our Father.

6 | follow up

During the week, do at least one of the following activities with your child:

1. Memorize Titus 2:11.
2. As a family, go to Mass on at least one extra day besides Sunday.
3. Write out the words to the Prayer of Abandonment (see Appendix) and pray it in the evening.

For the grace of God has appeared for the salvation of all men.
—Titus 2:11

notes

_____

_____

_____

_____

_____

_____

_____

Lesson 17

God Calls Us to Reconciliation

Lesson Focus | Although man had turned away from God, God never turned away from man. He kept loving us and planned a way to reconcile us to himself. Jesus' death and Resurrection made that reconciliation possible. To receive the grace Christ won for us, however, we must first receive the Sacrament of Baptism. Baptism washes away Original Sin from our soul, gives us the gift of sanctifying grace, and makes us God's adopted children. The mark our Baptism leaves on our soul is indelible. Nothing can remove it, not even mortal sin.

1 | begin

- Pray the Glory Be with your child.
- Show your child the list of baptismal promises in the Appendix of this book. Explain that on the day he was baptized, his parents and godparents made those promises for him.
- Read John 3:1–18 aloud.

2 | summarize

Summarize this week's lesson for your child:

Example: *When you were baptized, you received the sanctifying grace won for you by Christ on the Cross. You became God's adopted child, and nothing you do can ever change that.*

3 | review

Review this week's lesson by asking your child the following questions:

1. What does Baptism give us that is necessary for Salvation? (*Sanctifying grace.*)
2. What else does Baptism do? (*Gives us the theological virtues, removes Original Sin and any personal sin, makes us members of the Church, enables us to receive the other Sacraments, and leaves an indelible spiritual seal, marking us as Christ's.*)
3. What do we call spiritual Baptism received by a person who is sorry for his sins, has tried to live a good life, and would have received the Sacrament of Baptism had he known about it or been given the chance? (*Baptism of desire.*)
4. What do we call the Baptism of a person who dies defending the Faith even though he has not received the Sacrament of Baptism? (*Baptism of blood.*)
5. What are some of our duties once we are baptized? (*Live Sacramental lives, obey Church teaching, read Scripture, attend Mass, pray, do good works.*)

References

- Student Textbook: Chapter 17, pp. 92–96

- Sacred Scripture: Mt 3; 28:18–20; Lk 15:11–32; Jn 3:1–18; Rom 5:6–11; 2 Cor 5:17–21

- *Catechism of the Catholic Church*: 1213–85

4 | apply

Help your child apply this week's lesson by asking the following questions:
1. Of all the duties your Baptism requires of you, which is the easiest? The hardest? Why?
2. What more could you do to show God that you appreciate the gift of your Baptism?
3. How do you think you are different because of your Baptism? What might you be like if you had never been baptized and never knew who Jesus was?

5 | conclude

- With your child, pray the Our Father.

6 | follow up

During the week, do at least one of the following activities with your child:
1. Memorize John 3:5.
2. At night, include your child's godparents in your family prayers.
3. With your child, visit the baptismal font in your church. Look for symbols or imagery on or near it and discuss what those symbols might mean.

Jesus answered, "Truly, truly, I say to you, unless one is born of water and the Spirit, he cannot enter the kingdom of God."
—John 3:5

notes

_____

_____

_____

_____

_____

_____

_____

The Rite of Baptism

Lesson Focus | Through the events of salvation history, God's chosen people came to see water as a sign of God's promise to destroy evil and care for his children. John the Baptist also taught the Jews to see water as a sign of deliverance from sin. Water, as well as oil, fire, and a white garment are all important parts of the rite of Baptism. By our Baptism we are freed from personal sin and Original Sin and become God's adopted children.

1 | begin

- Pray the Glory Be with your child.
- Ask your child what water calls to mind. What does it do or help us to do?
- Read Matthew 3.

2 | summarize

Summarize this week's lesson for your child:

Example: *Throughout Salvation History, water has always been an important sign of healing, new life, and the destruction of evil. Through the rite of Baptism, it not only signifies those things; it actually accomplishes them.*

3 | review

Review this week's lesson by asking your child the following questions:

1. What are some examples of how the water of Baptism was prefigured in the Old Testament? (*In the flood, the parting of the Red Sea, the crossing of the Jordan, etc.*)
2. In Baptism, what does water signify? (*That we have been cleansed from sin.*)
3. What does the chrism oil signify? (*That we share in Christ's threefold ministry as priests, prophets, and kings.*)
4. What does the candle signify? (*That we've received Christ, the light of the world.*)
5. What does the white garment signify? (*That we are pure and clothed in Christ.*)
6. What do godparents do? (*Help the parents raise their child in the Catholic Faith.*)
7. What is an exorcism? (*A special Catholic ceremony that drives away the devil and destroys his influence.*)

References

- Student Textbook: Chapter 18, pp. 97–100

- Sacred Scripture: Gen 1:1 – 2:3, 6–7; Ex 14:14 – 15:3; Josh 1; 2 Kings 5:9–13; Mt 3; 28:18–19

- *Catechism of the Catholic Church:* 901–13, 1217–55, 1262–74

The Jordan River.

4 | apply

Help your child apply this week's lesson by asking the following questions:
1. How well do you think you're living out your baptismal promises? How could you do better?
2. Oil was often used to anoint athletes before a race. How is your Christian life like a race?
3. In what little ways does the devil try daily to lead you astray? How can you combat him?

5 | conclude

- With your child, pray the Our Father.

6 | follow up

During the week, do at least one of the following activities with your child:
1. Memorize Matthew 5:14.
2. Have your child write or call his godparents to talk about what he has learned this year in catechism class.
3. On each anniversary of your child's Baptism, have a celebration—a special dinner, cake, etc.—to mark the day he was born anew in Christ.

You are the light of the world. A city set on a hill cannot be hidden.
—Matthew 5:14

notes

_____

_____

_____

_____

_____

_____

_____

The Sacrament of Confirmation

Lesson Focus | At the Last Supper, Jesus promised to send the Holy Spirit to the Apostles to strengthen their faith and help them in the work of building his Church. The Holy Spirit came on Pentecost, ten days after Jesus' Ascension. All Christians receive the Holy Spirit at their Baptism. In the Sacrament of Confirmation, however, his power in our lives is strengthened. This Sacrament deepens and increases the sanctifying grace in our soul, equipping us with the special strength and gifts of the Holy Spirit that enable us to live our Christian faith better, in word and deed.

1 | begin

- Pray the Glory Be with your child.
- Ask your child what a soldier takes with him into battle or what a nurse takes with her when she goes to help people in a disaster zone.
- Read Acts 2:1–4 aloud.

2 | summarize

Summarize this week's lesson for your child:

Example: *Just as a soldier never goes into battle without his weapons, and a nurse never goes into a disaster zone without first-aid supplies, no Christian faces the challenges of life alone. The Holy Spirit is always with us—strengthening us, guiding us, and teaching us.*

3 | review

Review this week's lesson by asking your child the following questions:

1. Why is the Holy Spirit called a Paraclete, or the Advocate? (*A paraclete, or advocate, is someone who pleads before a judge on behalf of someone else. The Holy Spirit pleads for us and helps us pray.*)
2. What do wind and fire symbolize? (*Invisible power, enthusiasm, zeal, the flame of the missionary spirit, cleansing.*)
3. What is the sign of Confirmation? (*The laying on of hands and anointing with chrism.*)
4. What are the effects of Confirmation? (*A spiritual seal that deepens and increases sanctifying grace. It also makes us spiritual adults responsible for spreading the Faith.*)
5. Who is the usual minister of Confirmation? (*The bishop, but he can delegate to a priest.*)
6. When did Jesus promise to send the Holy Spirit? When did he fulfill that promise? (*The Last Supper; Pentecost.*)

References

- Student Textbook: Chapter 19, pp. 101–5

- Sacred Scripture: Acts 2:1–4

- *Catechism of the Catholic Church*: 692–701, 731–32, 1285–1321

4 | apply

Help your child apply this week's lesson by asking the following questions:
1. As you get older, what challenges will you face that you don't face now?
2. How do you think the Holy Spirit can help you face those challenges?
3. The Sacrament of Confirmation calls all Catholics to spread the Faith to others. Name someone you could talk to about the Faith or invite to youth group or church?

5 | conclude

- With your child, pray the Our Father.

6 | follow up

During the week, do at least one of the following activities with your child:
1. Memorize 2 Timothy 1:14.
2. Invite a non-Catholic friend to watch a movie with you about a saint or the Church.
3. Pray the Come, Holy Spirit prayer (see Appendix) before bed.

> *Guard the truth that has been entrusted to you by the Holy Spirit who dwells within us.*
> —2 Timothy 1:14

notes

_____

_____

_____

_____

_____

_____

_____

Lesson 20

The Gifts of the Holy Spirit

Lesson Focus | At our Confirmation, we receive an outpouring of the seven gifts of the Holy Spirit. These gifts help us live a life that is pleasing to God and give us joy. To use these gifts to their fullest, we must practice virtue and ask the Holy Spirit to help us use his gifts when we need them. The more we do this, the more the twelve fruits of the Holy Spirit will be evident in our life. The fruits are the effects of the seven gifts.

1 | begin

- Pray the Glory Be with your child.
- Ask your child what happens when a person works hard to use his natural gifts in school, sports, music, etc.
- Read Isaiah 11:2 aloud.

2 | summarize

Summarize this week's lesson for your child:

Example: *When someone uses his gifts of intelligence or athletic ability, he succeeds. His success is the fruit of his work. The same is true in the spiritual life. When we work hard to use the gifts of the Spirit, the fruit of that is evident in our life.*

3 | review

Review this week's lesson by asking your child the following questions:

1. Name and define each of the seven gifts of the Holy Spirit. (*1. Wisdom—the ability to see things as God sees them; 2. Understanding—insight into the mysteries of faith; 3. Knowledge—the ability to see everything in relation to God and eternity; 4. Counsel—the ability to make correct decisions about God's will for our lives; 5. Fortitude—the strength to be faithful to Christ when it's difficult; 6. Piety—the inspiration to worship God and love him as Father; 7. Fear of the Lord—the ability to see the evil of sin and the goodness of God.*)
2. What are the twelve fruits of the Holy Spirit? (*Charity, joy, peace, patience, kindness, goodness, generosity, gentleness, faithfulness, modesty, self-control, and chastity.*)
3. How can we increase the power of the Holy Spirit's gifts in our life? (*Ask him to help us use the gifts in times of need.*)

References

- Student Textbook: Chapter 20, pp. 106–8
- Sacred Scripture: Is 11:2; Jn 14:23
- *Catechism of the Catholic Church*: 733–36, 768, 798–801, 1285–1321, 1830–32

4 | apply

Help your child apply this week's lesson by asking the following questions:

1. Can you give me an example of a time you've used each of the Spirit's seven gifts?
2. Which of the fruits do you see in your life? Which don't you see, or of which do you see little?
3. Which of the seven gifts do you need to ask for the Holy Spirit's help in using?

5 | conclude

- With your child, pray the Our Father.

6 | follow up

During the week, do at least one of the following activities with your child:

1. Memorize Matthew 7:16.
2. Encourage your child to pray nightly for an outpouring of the gifts of the Holy Spirit that he most needs or wants.
3. Learn about Saint Teresa of Avila or Saint John of the Cross. What challenges did they face? What gifts of the Holy Spirit did they manifest most powerfully? What fruits came out of their lives and work?

> *You will know them by their fruits. Are grapes gathered from thorns, or figs from thistles?*
> —Matthew 7:16

notes

_____

_____

_____

_____

_____

_____

_____

Lesson 21

The Sacrament of the Holy Eucharist

Lesson Focus | At the Last Supper, Jesus revealed how it would be possible for his followers to eat his Flesh and drink his Blood. There, for the first time, he changed bread and wine into his Body and Blood, instituting the Sacrament of the Eucharist. In the Mass, when the priest repeats Jesus' words from the Last Supper the substance of the bread and wine changes, even though the appearance does not; this is called transubstantiation. The Eucharist is our spiritual food. It helps us grow in holiness and deepens our love for Jesus. We should try to receive it often, always worthily, and daily if possible.

1 | begin

- Pray the Glory Be with your child.
- Ask your child what would happen to him if he stopped eating. What effect would that have on his body? His attitude? His life?
- Read John 6:35–66 aloud.

2 | summarize

Summarize this week's lesson for your child:

Example: *Just as our bodies would grow sick and weak without food, our souls would grow sick and weak without the Eucharist. The Eucharist is Christ's Body and Blood. Every time we receive it, we receive him, his life, which nourishes our souls and deepens our love for him.*

3 | review

Review this week's lesson by asking your child the following questions:

1. Define *transubstantiation*. (*The changing of bread and wine into the Body, Blood, Soul, and Divinity of Jesus.*)
2. Define *Real Presence*. (*The fact that Jesus is really and truly present in the Holy Eucharist under the appearance of bread and wine.*)
3. Define *tabernacle*. (*The special, solid, immovable container in which the Eucharist is kept.*)
4. Define *sacrilege*. (*Serious mistreatment of people, places, or things consecrated to God. Receiving Holy Communion while in the state of mortal sin is a sacrilege.*)
5. How do we know Jesus is present in the Eucharist? (*By faith in his words, not by sight.*)
6. What does Holy Communion do? (*Gives us grace, forgives our venial sins, helps us avoid sin, deepens our love for Jesus, increases our joy and hope, eases our sorrow.*)

References

- Student Textbook: Chapter 21, pp. 109–14
- Sacred Scripture: Mt 14:14–21; 26:26–28; Lk 22:19–20; Jn 6:1–15, 35–69; 1 Cor 11:23–24
- *Catechism of the Catholic Church*: 1322–1419, 2120

4 | apply

Help your child apply this week's lesson by asking the following questions:

1. If you had been present when Jesus spoke the words we read from John how would you have reacted? Why do you think so many left? Why do you think some stayed?
2. What makes it possible for you to believe that the Eucharist is really Jesus?
3. How do you think going to Mass on more than just Sundays could help you?

5 | conclude

■ With your child, pray the Our Father.

6 | follow up

During the week, do at least one of the following activities with your child:

1. Memorize John 6:35.
2. Learn about one of the great Eucharistic miracles at Orvieto, Lanciano, or Sienna.
3. As a family, go to Mass on at least one extra day besides Sunday.

Jesus said to them, "I am the bread of life; he who comes to me shall not hunger; and he who believes in me shall never thirst."
—John 6:35

notes

_____

_____

_____

_____

_____

_____

_____

The Eucharistic Sacrifice

Lesson Focus | The Eucharist is more than a sacred meal. It is also a holy sacrifice. It is, in fact, the same sacrifice that took place on Calvary. On Calvary, Jesus offered himself on the altar of the Cross. In the Mass, Jesus continues to offer himself, through his priest, to the Father. At the Last Supper, Jesus made clear the connection between the two seemingly different sacrifices—telling us that the bread was his Body "given up" and the wine his Blood that would be "poured out"—but how this is possible is still a mystery of faith.

1 | begin

- Pray the Glory Be with your child.
- Ask your child if he has ever heard anyone say, "I don't get anything out of Mass." What could a person mean by that? What does it say about the way that person thinks of Mass?
- Read 1 Corinthians 11:23–26 aloud.

2 | summarize

Summarize this week's lesson for your child:

Example: *The primary reason we go to Mass is not for what we "get" out of it. The Mass is not about us. It's about Christ and what we give to him as we participate in his perpetual sacrifice of himself to the Father. In the Mass, we stand with Mary at the foot of the Cross.*

References

- Student Textbook: Chapter 22, pp. 115–18

- Sacred Scripture: Mal 1:11; Lk 24:13–25; Jn 18–19; 1 Cor 11:26; Heb 13:8

- *Catechism of the Catholic Church*: 1322–1419, 2096–2100, 2177–83

3 | review

Review this week's lesson by asking your child the following questions:

1. How is the Mass a meal? (*The Mass looks like a meal because it has a "table" [altar] with bread and wine and people eating and praying together.*)
2. How is the Mass a sacrifice? (*It has an altar, a victim, and a priest. It is the one perfect sacrifice of Christ made present to us.*)
3. Although the two events are the same, what are the main differences between the Mass and the Cross? (*1. On the Cross, Jesus' sacrifice was bloody and painful. In the Mass, it's not. 2. On the Cross, Jesus offered himself by himself. In the Mass, he offers himself through the priest and with the whole Church.*)
4. In the Mass, when does the Consecration occur? (*When the priest says Jesus' words from the Last Supper: "This is my Body" and "This is the chalice of my Blood."*)
5. What happens with those words? (*Bread and wine become Jesus' Body and Blood.*)

4 | apply

Help your child apply this week's lesson by asking the following questions:

1. If you had stood with Mary at the foot of the Cross, how would you have felt?
2. How does knowing that the sacrifice of the Mass is the same sacrifice as Calvary affect the way you think and feel about the Mass? What does that knowledge ask of you?
3. In what two or three ways can you prepare yourself for Mass?

5 | conclude

- With your child, pray the Our Father.

6 | follow up

During the week, do at least one of the following activities with your child:

1. Memorize Hebrews 13:8.
2. As a family, read the Sunday Mass readings on Saturday night.
3. Arrive at Sunday Mass five to ten minutes early so your family will have time to pray beforehand.

> *Jesus Christ is the same yesterday and today and for ever.*
> —Hebrews 13:8

notes

_____

_____

_____

_____

_____

_____

_____

Lesson 23

The Eucharist in Our Lives

Lesson Focus | The Eucharist is often referred to as the "source and summit" of the Christian life and the "greatest of the Sacraments." This is because Christ himself is really and truly present in the Eucharist. The other Sacraments lead us to Christ and deepen our faith in him. The Eucharist *is* Christ. We will receive the spiritual benefits of the Eucharist, however, only if we receive it worthily, knowing whom we're receiving, believing in it, free from mortal sin, and observing the Eucharistic fast.

1 | begin

- Pray the Glory Be with your child.
- Ask your child if a friend has ever rejected him—by either not being kind to him or not wanting to spending time with him. How did that feel?
- Read Matthew 26:20—29 aloud.

2 | summarize

Summarize this week's lesson for your child:

Example: *To receive the Eucharist unworthily, not to care about it, and never to show reverence to Jesus in the Eucharist is to reject the great gift he gives us. It is to do to him what your friend did to you. Judas did that at the Last Supper—eating, then leaving to betray Jesus.*

3 | review

Review this week's lesson by asking your child the following questions:

1. Why is the Eucharist the source and summit of the Christian life? (*Because it is Christ, who is the source of our faith, and being with him is the goal of our life.*)
2. What does it mean to receive the Eucharist worthily? (*1. To be free from serious sin; 2. To believe in the Real Presence; 3. To have fasted for one hour from food and drink.*)
3. How is the Eucharist related to the other Sacraments? (*Baptism: makes us members of the Church so we can receive the Eucharist; Confirmation: gives us the gifts of the Holy Spirit, which help us to know Jesus in the Eucharist; Penance: takes away our sins so we can receive Jesus with pure hearts; Anointing of the Sick: strengthens us and prepares those about to receive the Eucharist for the last time on earth; Holy Orders: gives us priests who will celebrate the Eucharist for us; Matrimony: husband and wife are called to give themselves to each other as Christ gives himself to us in the Eucharist.*)

References

- Student Textbook: Chapter 23, pp. 119–22
- Sacred Scripture: Mt 26:1–29
- *Catechism of the Catholic Church*: 1322–1419, 1524–25

4 | apply

Help your child apply this week's lesson by asking the following questions:
1. How can you show reverence for the Eucharist during Mass?
2. How can you show reverence for the Eucharist outside of Mass?
3. How can spending time with Jesus in the Eucharist outside of Mass help you?

5 | conclude

- With your child, pray the Our Father.

6 | follow up

During the week, do at least one of the following activities with your child:
1. Memorize Philippians 2:10.
2. Spend thirty minutes this week in prayer before the Blessed Sacrament.
3. Go to confession as a family sometime this week.

At the name of Jesus every knee should bow, in heaven and on earth and under the earth.
—Philippians 2:10

notes

_____

_____

_____

_____

_____

_____

_____

Lesson 24

Sin and Mankind

Lesson Focus | All sin is an offense against God, and all sin has consequences. Original Sin, the sin inherited from our first parents, is removed through Baptism, but it leaves us susceptible to other sins. Mortal sin kills the life of grace in our souls. Venial sin diminishes the life of grace in us and makes it more likely that we will commit serious sin. To avoid hurting ourselves and offending God, we need to recognize possible sources of temptation, avoid near occasions of sin, and form our consciences in accord with the truth.

1 | begin

- Pray the Glory Be with your child.
- Tell your child about a time you deliberately chose to do something wrong (e.g., lie, disobey your parents, not be kind to someone, etc.) and what led you to make that choice.
- Read Romans 7:15–19 aloud.

2 | summarize

Summarize this week's lesson for your child:

Example: *What Paul describes is a struggle we all face daily. Our fallen nature inclines us to sin, to do what we know is wrong, hurting ourselves, others, and God.*

3 | review

Review this week's lesson by asking your child the following questions:

1. What are the two kinds of actual sin? (*Mortal: destroys the life of grace; venial: diminishes it.*)
2. In what four ways can sins be committed? (*In thought, word, deed, omission.*)
3. What are the conditions for mortal sin? (*Grave matter, full knowledge, full consent.*)
4. What is a near occasion of sin? (*A person, place, thing, or circumstance that tempts us to sin or puts us in danger of sinning.*)
5. What are the seven capital sins? (*Pride, avarice/greed, envy, wrath/uncontrolled anger, lust, gluttony, sloth/laziness.*)
6. How do we form our consciences properly? (*By studying the teachings of the Church.*)

References

- Student Textbook: Chapter 24, pp. 123–26
- Sacred Scripture: 2:15; 7:15–19
- *Catechism of the Catholic Church*: 1422–98, 1783–89, 1849–66

4 | apply

Help your child apply this week's lesson by asking the following questions:

1. Can you give me an example of a near occasion of sin? What are some persons, places, or things you need to avoid in order to avoid certain sins?
2. Give me an example of the harmful consequences of sin that you've seen in your own life or in another's.
3. Temptations to sin come to us from the world, the flesh, and the devil. What's an example of a temptation of the world? The flesh? The devil?

5 | conclude

- With your child, pray the Our Father.

6 | follow up

During the week, do at least one of the following activities with your child:

1. Memorize Romans 7:19.
2. Together, look through a newspaper or magazine for messages that can be a source of temptation to sin.
3. Encourage your child to pray the Prayer to Saint Michael (see Appendix) when faced with temptation.

> *For I do not do the good I want, but the evil I do not want is what I do.*
> —Romans 7:19

notes

_____

_____

_____

_____

_____

_____

_____

Lesson 25

God's Mercy and Forgiveness

Lesson Focus | Although God hates sin, he loves us. He is full of mercy and is ready to and wants to forgive us for our sins. No sin is too big for him to forgive. We must never forget his mercy and love and should strive to be loving toward everyone, even those who have sinned against us. We should also regularly examine our consciences to see where we've fallen, regularly go to confession, to receive both forgiveness and strength not to sin again, and do small penances to help make up for the damage our sin causes.

1 | begin

- Pray the Glory Be with your child.
- Talk to your child about how sad it makes you when he disobeys you and that even when you get angry, it's only because you love him and want what's best for him.
- Read Luke 7:41–50 aloud.

2 | summarize

Summarize this week's lesson for your child:

Example: *During his life on earth, Jesus showed us that God is a loving Father. He hates sin, but one of the reasons he hates it is because it hurts us. He never stops loving us when we sin and is always ready and wanting to forgive us when we come to him.*

3 | review

Review this week's lesson by asking your child the following questions:
1. What is perfect contrition? (*Sorrow for sin caused by love of God.*)
2. What is imperfect contrition? (*Sorrow for sin caused by fear of hell.*)
3. Define *examination of conscience*. (*Thinking about what sins we have committed and why, so that we can avoid those sins in the future and prepare for the Sacrament of Penance.*)
4. What is penance and what does it do for us? (*Acts of self-denial that strengthen our will and make it easier for us to avoid sin in the future.*)
5. What is a purpose of amendment? (*A firm commitment to sin no more.*)
6. How did Jesus treat sinners? (*He hated the sin but loved the sinner, calling people to repentance but still loving them, being kind to them, talking to them, and wanting what was best for them.*)

References

- Student Textbook: Chapter 25, pp. 127–30

- Sacred Scripture: Ps 34; 103; 145; Lk 7:41–50; 13:34; 15:11–32; Jn 8:1–11; 1 Jn 4

- *Catechism of the Catholic Church*: 1424–58, 1776–1802, 1846–48

4 | apply

Help your child apply this week's lesson by asking the following questions:

1. What can you learn from Jesus about how you should treat those in serious sin?
2. Have you ever been afraid to confess something to God? Why? Does it help to know there's nothing he can't forgive (and that the priest has already heard someone else confess the same sin)? How?
3. What are some small acts of penance you can do to strengthen your will?

5 | conclude

- With your child, pray the Our Father.

6 | follow up

During the week, do at least one of the following activities with your child:

1. Memorize Matthew 18:7.
2. Encourage your child to do an examination of conscience every evening before bed.
3. In the evening, pray together Psalm 51, the great psalm of repentance.

> *Woe to the world for temptations to sin! For it is necessary that temptations come, but woe to the man by whom the temptation comes!*
> —Matthew 18:7

notes

_____

_____

_____

_____

_____

_____

_____

The Sacrament of Penance

Lesson Focus | In the evening of the day he rose from the dead, Jesus gave his Apostles the power to forgive sins in his name. They handed this power on to their successors, the bishops, who in turn share it with their helpers, priests. When we go to a priest, confess our sins, express true repentance, and receive absolution, our sins are forgiven. Also, some of the punishment we deserve for our sin is taken away, and we receive grace to help us avoid sin in the future. This is why we should go to confession frequently, not just when we commit mortal sins.

1 | begin

- Pray the Glory Be with your child.
- Ask your child who is hurt when we commit sins (e.g., ourselves, those we involve in our sins or sin against, those who love us, the culture, and above all, God.)
- Read John 20:19–23 aloud.

2 | summarize

Summarize this week's lesson for your child:

Example: *Jesus had the power to forgive sin because he is God and all sins are, in some way, against God. So that we could receive his forgiveness after his Ascension, he shared that power with his Apostles and their successors. They use that power in the Sacrament of Penance.*

3 | review

Review this week's lesson by asking your child the following questions:

1. What five elements are part of every good Confession? (*1. Examination of conscience; 2. Sorrow for having sinned; 3. A firm resolution not to sin in the future and to avoid near occasions of sin; 4. Confession of all our sins, venial and mortal, to a priest; 5. Receiving absolution and completing the assigned penance.*)
2. What is the sign of the Sacrament of Penance? (*Confessing sins to a priest and the words of absolution.*)
3. Who is the minister of this Sacrament? (*The priest.*)
4. What are the effects? (*Forgiveness of sin, grace to sin no more.*)

References

- Student Textbook: Chapter 26, pp. 131–36
- Sacred Scripture: Mt 18:23–25; Lk 5:18–25; Jn 20:19–23
- *Catechism of the Catholic Church*: 1422–98

4 | apply

Help your child apply this week's lesson by asking the following questions:
1. What do you like most about going to confession?
2. What do you like least about going to confession?
3. What is a virtue you're struggling to develop, a vice you're trying to overcome, or a difficulty you're trying to face, with which the graces of confession could help you?

5 | conclude

- With your child, pray the Our Father.

6 | follow up

During the week, do at least one of the following activities with your child:
1. Memorize 1 John 1:9.
2. If your child didn't go to confession with his class, go as a family.
3. Learn about Saint Augustine and his conversion. Talk about how his personal struggle with sin made it difficult for him to convert, but what a great saint he became once he gave his life to Christ.

The true light that enlightens every man was coming into the world.
—John 1:9

notes

_____

_____

_____

_____

_____

_____

_____

The Sacrament of the Anointing of the Sick

Lesson Focus | When Jesus was on earth, he cured many people who were ill or infirm. He also shared this healing power with his Apostles. Today, the Church continues to heal people in body or soul, or both, through the Sacrament of the Anointing of the Sick. The Sacrament is administered by a priest when someone is seriously ill in mind or body. It can bring physical healing, but more often it gives the grace to suffer with peace and courage. It also can prepare a person for death, but it is not a Sacrament just for the dying.

1 | begin

- Pray the Glory Be with your child.
- Ask your child how he would feel if he learned he was very sick. Would he be scared? Would he wonder why he was sick? Would he ask Jesus for healing?
- Read John 5:1–5 aloud.

2 | summarize

Summarize this week's lesson for your child:

Example: *After Jesus had ascended into heaven, he continued to heal bodies and strengthen souls through the Sacrament of the Anointing of the Sick. Those who are very sick receive that Sacrament because it helps them to have courage, suffer well, trust God, and sometimes be healed physically.*

3 | review

Review this week's lesson by asking your child the following questions:

1. What is the main purpose of this Sacrament? (*To strengthen a person who is suffering and prepare his soul for possible death.*)
2. What does the Sacrament do? (*Increases sanctifying grace and gives spiritual strength to resist temptation, bear evil, and die a holy death. It takes away venial and mortal sins if the person is sorry for them. It also can restore bodily health if that is God's will.*)
3. Who is the minister of the Sacrament? (*The priest.*)
4. What is the Sacrament's sign? (*Anointing with the oil of the sick and the priest's prayer.*)
5. What is the difference between a plenary and a partial indulgence? (*A plenary indulgence removes all temporal punishment due to sin; a partial indulgence removes some.*)
6. What are the conditions for obtaining a plenary indulgence? (*Be in a state of grace, be detached from sin, do the prescribed good work, pray for the Pope, receive Holy Communion, and go to Confession.*)

References

- Student Textbook: Chapter 27, pp. 137–42
- Sacred Scripture: Mt 9:1–8; Mk 6:7, 12–13; 7:31–37; Jn 4:46–54, Jas 4:14–15
- *Catechism of the Catholic Church*: 1499–1532

4 | apply

Help your child apply this week's lesson by asking the following questions:
1. Why do you think God heals only some people?
2. How can you prepare yourself now for a good death?
3. What do you think could help you face death unafraid?

5 | conclude

- With your child, pray the Our Father.

6 | follow up

During the week, do at least one of the following activities with your child:
1. Memorize Psalm 41:3.
2. At night, pray the Prayer to Saint Joseph for a Happy Death (see Appendix).
3. Find out if there is a shrine or a chapel in your area where a plenary indulgence can be obtained. If so, go to Mass there as a family and pray the prescribed prayers.

> *The LORD sustains him on his sickbed; in his illness you heal all his infirmities.*
> —Psalm 41:3

notes

_____

_____

_____

_____

_____

_____

_____

The Sacrament of Holy Orders

Lesson Focus | At the Last Supper, Jesus gave his Apostles a share in his own ministerial priesthood. This meant they could celebrate Mass, hear confessions, and administer the other Sacraments, as well as proclaim his Word with special authority. To be a priest is to be a spiritual father, and it is a calling that must come from God. When a man is ordained, he receives the power to share in Christ's priesthood and all the grace he needs to serve God and grow in holiness.

1 | begin

- Pray the Glory Be with your child.
- Ask your child who his favorite priest or deacon is. What does he like about him? How does he see Christ in him?
- Read Luke 22:1–19 aloud.

2 | summarize

Summarize this week's lesson for your child:

Example: *At the Last Supper, Jesus instituted two Sacraments: the Eucharist and Holy Orders. Holy Orders gives the men whom God calls to the priesthood or diaconate the grace to be spiritual fathers. They share in Christ's priesthood and continue his work in the world.*

3 | review

Review this week's lesson by asking your child the following questions:

1. What are the three degrees of Holy Orders? (*Bishop, priest, deacon.*)
2. Explain the ministry of each. (*Bishops are the official teachers and sanctifiers of the faithful in a diocese; priests help the bishop by preaching, teaching, and administering Sacraments; deacons serve the Church through good works and assisting at Mass.*)
3. What is apostolic succession? (*The unbroken chain of bishops from the Apostles to the present day.*)
4. What is the priesthood of the faithful? (*The priesthood of all Catholics, including religious brothers and sisters, carried out by attending Mass and worshipping God in prayer.*)
5. What is the Sacramental seal for Holy Orders? (*The spiritual mark on the soul of one ordained to Holy Orders, similar to the mark left by Baptism and Confirmation.*)

References

- Student Textbook: Chapter 28, pp. 143–47
- Sacred Scripture: Lk 22:1–19; Acts 6:1–6
- *Catechism of the Catholic Church*: 783–84, 871–903, 1536–1600

4 | apply

Help your child apply this week's lesson by asking the following questions:

1. How do you think it helps the Church to have men who have dedicated their whole lives to serving the Church?
2. How do you think we can help our priests serve the Church?
3. (To a boy:) Have you ever thought God might be calling you to the priesthood?
4. (To a girl:) Have you ever thought God might be calling you to consecrated religious life?

5 | conclude

- With your child, pray the Our Father.

6 | follow up

During the week, do at least one of the following activities with your child:

1. Memorize 1 Peter 2:9.
2. Pray for your priest and bishop during your family's evening prayers.
3. Invite your pastor or associate pastor to join your family for dinner.

But you are a chosen race, a royal priesthood, a holy nation, God's own people, that you may declare the wonderful deeds of him who called you out of darkness into his marvelous light.
—1 Peter 2:9

notes

_____

_____

_____

_____

_____

_____

_____

The Sacrament of Matrimony

Lesson Focus | Marriage is the first relationship any two humans ever entered into with each other. In the garden, God gave Adam and Eve to each other in marriage. He also revealed there the twofold purpose of marriage: mutual love and procreation. Married couples are called to help each other in this life and to grow in holiness. They also are called to be open to accepting the children God sends them and to raise those children well. They are to be faithful to each other and recognize that marriage is a lifelong bond.

1 | begin

- Pray the Glory Be with your child.
- Show your child a picture of you (or your parents or dear friends) on your wedding day.
- Read Genesis 2:18–25 aloud.

2 | summarize

Summarize this week's lesson for your child:

Example: *God made man and woman for each other. In marriage, we're called to love each other, support each other, and help each other become holy. We're also called to be open to life and raise children.*

3 | review

Review this week's lesson by asking your child the following questions:

1. What are the main purposes of the covenant of marriage? (*The good of the spouses and the procreation and education of children.*)
2. What does the grace of the Sacrament of Matrimony do? (*It helps the spouses assist one another in growing in holiness and in welcoming and educating their children.*)
3. Define *mutual love.* (*One of the purposes of marriage; the duty of the husband and wife to love, serve, and support each other and help each other to know, love, and serve God.*)
4. Define *procreation.* (*Another purpose of marriage; the cooperation of the husband and wife with God in bringing new life into the world.*)
5. What is necessary for a valid Christian marriage? (*The couple must be free to make their vows and agree to live their marriage in accord with God's plan and the Church's rules.*)
6. Why is it impossible to end a valid marriage? (*In a valid marriage, husband and wife become one flesh and a symbol of Christ's love for the Church, and Christ can never be separated from his Church.*)

References

- Student Textbook: Chapter 29, pp. 148–51

- Sacred Scripture: Gen 2:18, 21–25; Mt 19:4–12; Jn 2:1–11

- *Catechism of the Catholic Church*: 1601–66, 2360–91

4 | apply

Help your child apply this week's lesson by asking the following questions:
1. How is the culture making it harder for people to have strong and lasting marriages?
2. What are some things you can do now to start preparing yourself to have a strong Christian marriage, if that's the vocation to which God calls you?
3. Whose marriage do you admire? What do you admire about it?

5 | conclude

- With your child, pray the Our Father.

6 | follow up

During the week, do at least one of the following activities with your child:
1. Memorize Ephesians 5:25.
2. Invite a young married couple or an older married couple to your house for dinner.
3. Learn about Saint Thérèse's parents, Blessed Louis and Zélie Martin. Ask for their prayers for the married couples you know.

Husbands, love your wives, as Christ loved the Church and gave himself up for her.
—Ephesians 5:25

notes

_____

_____

_____

_____

_____

_____

_____

Lesson 30

Sacramentals

Lesson Focus | The Sacraments are the primary means by which Catholics receive grace and grow in faith. Two other means are sacramentals and acts of popular piety. Sacramentals prepare us to receive grace through the Sacraments and may also give us grace by the prayer of the Church, who instituted them. Acts of piety are acts of reverence toward God or his saints. These can include special devotions, prayers, and gestures that are little ways of expressing love for God and growing closer to him through that expression.

1 | begin

- Pray the Glory Be with your child.
- Talk to your child about special traditions or habits your family enjoys together that have brought you closer as a family (e.g., Sunday drives, family movie nights, etc.).
- Read Ephesians 1:3 aloud.

2 | summarize

Summarize this week's lesson for your child:

Example: *In the family of God, we also have traditions that help dispose us to receive grace, enabling us to love God and one another better. We call these traditions and acts of piety sacramentals.*

3 | review

Review this week's lesson by asking your child the following questions:

1. Define *Sacrament*. (*A visible sign instituted by Christ to confer grace.*)
2. Define *sacramental*. (*A sign that, through the prayers of the Church, prepares people to receive grace.*)
3. Who instituted the Sacraments? The sacramentals? (*Christ; the Church.*)
4. What is popular piety? (*The way people express their personal reverence or devotion to God or the saints.*)
5. What are examples of sacramentals? (*Answers might include: candles, incense, holy water, blessings, the Rosary, etc.*)
6. What are some examples of acts of piety? (*Answers might include: novenas, prayers to specific saints, visits to shrines, reverence for relics, the Divine Mercy Chaplet, etc.*)

References

- Student Textbook: Chapter 30, pp. 152–54

- Sacred Scripture: Lk 6:28; Rom 12:14; Eph 1:3; 1 Pet 3:9

- *Catechism of the Catholic Church:* 1667–76

4 | apply

Help your child apply this week's lesson by asking the following questions:

1. Do you have a favorite sacramental? What is it? Why is it your favorite?
2. Do you have a favorite saint or devotion? Who or what is it? Why?
3. How could the use of sacramentals or devotions be misused? How can we avoid misusing them?

5 | conclude

- With your child, pray the Our Father.

6 | follow up

During the week, do at least one of the following activities with your child:

1. Pray a Rosary or Divine Mercy Chaplet (see Appendix) together.
2. Learn about Our Lady of Guadalupe and her appearance to Saint Juan Diego.
3. Visit a nearby Catholic shrine, and attend Mass there.

notes

_____

_____

_____

_____

_____

_____

_____

Lesson 31

Mary, Mediatrix of Grace

Lesson Focus | Mary is often called the mediatrix of grace because all grace comes to us from Jesus, and Jesus came to us through Mary. She is our Mother in faith, who gave birth to the Son of God and prays for us as her own children. She also, by her example on earth, teaches us how to follow Jesus perfectly. Mary wasn't only Jesus' Mother; she was his most perfect disciple. For all those reasons, Jesus asks us to love Mary as our own Mother and go to her with all our needs, big and small.

1 | begin

- Pray the Glory Be with your child.
- Tell your child about a time you turned to Mary in your need or about a lesson you learned from reading about her in the Gospels.
- Read John 19:25–27 aloud.

2 | summarize

Summarize this week's lesson for your child:

Example: *Jesus wants us to love and honor Mary as our own Mother because she gave him life. She brought the source of all grace into the world and was his most perfect disciple. We learn how to love Jesus better by imitating Mary and relying on her whenever we're in need.*

3 | review

Review this week's lesson by asking your child the following questions:

1. Define *mediatrix*. (*A title for Mary that reminds us that Jesus came to us through her and that she now prays to Jesus for us.*)
2. What does it mean to consecrate ourselves to Mary? (*To give ourselves entirely to Mary so she can help us to become like Jesus.*)
3. What four privileges did God give to Mary? (*1. The Immaculate Conception—Mary was preserved from Original Sin from the moment of her conception. 2. Perpetual virginity—Mary remained a virgin before, during, and after Jesus' birth; 3. The Assumption—Mary was assumed, body and soul, into heaven at the end of her earthly life; 4. Mother of God—Mary is truly the Mother of God because she is the Mother of Christ, true God and true man.*)

References

- Student Textbook: Chapter 31, pp. 155–57

- Sacred Scripture: Lk 1:26 — 2:52; 24:1–11; Jn 2:1–11; 19:25–27; Acts 1:1–11

- *Catechism of the Catholic Church*: 490–507, 963–70, 2617–19, 2673–79

4 | apply

Help your child apply this week's lesson by asking the following questions:

1. Why do you think it doesn't take any honor away from Jesus when we honor Mary?
2. Do you think of Mary as your Mother? Why or why not?
3. With what has Mary helped you? When could you have turned to her but didn't? How could turning to her have made a difference?

5 | conclude

- With your child, pray the Our Father.

6 | follow up

During the week, do at least one of the following activities with your child:

1. Memorize John 2:5.
2. Encourage your child to dramatize with friends some key events of Mary's life or to put on a play in which Mary speaks to people who are facing a great struggle or moral dilemma.
3. Memorize the short Prayer of Consecration to Mary (see Appendix).

> *His mother said to the servants, "Do whatever he tells you."*
> —John 2:5

notes

_____

_____

_____

_____

_____

_____

_____

Our Life in the Church

Grade 8

According to the riches of his glory he may grant you to be strengthened with might through his Spirit in the inner man, and that Christ may dwell in your hearts through faith . . . to him be glory in the Church and in Christ Jesus to all generations, for ever and ever. Amen.

Ephesians 3:16–17, 21

Christ's Abiding Presence

Lesson Focus | The Gospels tell us that Christ founded the Church. Through her, he is with us always. The Apostles received from him the authority to make decisions, proclaim the gospel, administer the Sacraments, and forgive sins. Christ also established a hierarchy to govern the Church and set rules. Because Christ founded her and is her head, and because the Holy Spirit guides her, the Church is a divine institution. Although her members are human, she isn't something men have made, and men don't have authority to change her.

1 | begin

- Pray the Glory Be with your child.
- Ask your child what it means to love someone. If you knew that someone you love needed you, would you leave that person alone? Would you abandon that person?
- Read Matthew 16:13–20 aloud.

2 | summarize

Summarize this week's lesson for your child:

Example: *Jesus loves each and every one of us so much that he would have died for each of us alone. He would never abandon us. That's why he gave us the Church. Through her, he is with us always.*

3 | review

Review this week's lesson by asking your child the following questions:

1. How do we know Jesus intended to found the Church? (*He told the Apostles he would found his Church on Peter, and he talked about the authority the Church would have.*)
2. Why did Jesus found the Church? (*To shepherd his people and be with us always.*)
3. How is the Church human? (*She is made up of and governed by human beings.*)
4. How is the Church divine? (*Christ is her founder and head; she is of divine origin, and she has divine guidance and authority.*)
5. How is Christ present in his Church? (*In the Eucharist; in the authority given to the Pope and the bishops; in the person of the priest, who acts "in persona Christi"; in her members who have been baptized and who conform themselves to him, etc.*)

References

- Student Textbook: Chapter 1, pp. 11–14

- Sacred Scripture: Mt 3:13–19; 16:13–20; Jn 21:10–19; Acts 1:1 — 2:4; 1 Cor 12:12–27

- *Catechism of the Catholic Church*: 669, 787–96

4 | apply

Help your child apply this week's lesson by asking the following questions:

1. In other organizations, members vote on the rules and what the organization believes. But not the Church. Why do you think this is? What problems would arise if Catholics got to vote on what the Church teaches? How would that compromise Her mission?
2. What do you think your role in the Church is right now? What could it be someday?
3. We're called to see Christ in one another, as well as in the Church's priests and bishops. How hard is that? What does that mean for how we should treat one another?

5 | conclude

- With your child, pray the Our Father.

6 | follow up

During the week, do at least one of the following activities with your child:

1. Memorize Matthew 28:20.
2. Pray Saint Augustine's prayer to the Holy Spirit (see Appendix).
3. Pay a short visit to your parish's Adoration Chapel or tabernacle.

Teaching them to observe all that I have commanded you; and behold, I am with you always, to the close of the age.
—Matthew 28:20

notes

_____

_____

_____

_____

_____

_____

_____

The Birth of the Church

Lesson Focus | Ten days after he ascended into heaven, Jesus sent the Holy Spirit to his Apostles. This day, called Pentecost, is considered the birthday of the Church. It is the day on which the Church was made known to the world. Long before Pentecost, however, God began the work of building the Church. She was prefigured in the Old Testament by Israel and made manifest on earth when Christ was born.

1 | begin

- Pray the Glory Be with your child.
- Look up online the number of Catholics in various countries around the world. If you can, find a map showing the concentration of Catholics in various countries.
- Read Acts 2:1–11 aloud.

2 | summarize

Summarize this week's lesson for your child:

Example: *The coming of the Holy Spirit was, in a way, the beginning of the Church. Pentecost was the origin in space and time of a Church that covers the entire globe. But that day was also an end—an end to God's work of preparing the world for his Church.*

3 | review

Review this week's lesson by asking your child the following questions:

1. Define *deposit of grace*. (*All the grace necessary for salvation, which Jesus merited for us by His death and Resurrection, and which is given to us through the Church.*)
2. Define *deposit of Faith*. (*The content of revelation entrusted to the Church by Jesus and handed on through Scripture and Tradition by the Apostles and their successors.*)
3. Define *vicar*. (*A representative; one serving as an agent for someone else.*)
4. Define *ekklesia*. (*Greek word for "assembly"; used in the New Testament for "church."*)
5. What are the three stages for God's establishment of the Church? (*1. In the Old Testament, the Church is prefigured in God's promises to Adam, Abraham, Noah, and Moses, the nation of Israel, and the kingdom of David; 2. In his life and death, Jesus laid the foundation for his Church; 3. From Pentecost forward, the Apostles and their successors have had authority from Jesus to spread the gospel to all men.*)

References

- Student Textbook: Chapter 2, pp. 15–18
- Sacred Scripture: Gen 3:15; 9:8–11; 17; Ex 3—25; 28:40; 2 Sam 22; Mt 21:1–9; Acts 2:1–11
- *Catechism of the Catholic Church*: 54–55, 62–63, 84, 128–30, 731–41, 758–69, 2003

4 | apply

Help your child apply this week's lesson by asking the following questions:
1. What similarities do you see between the nation of Israel and the Catholic Church?
2. Do you think the Church could have endured intact through so many centuries and spread to so many places without God's help? Why or why not?
3. How can you help the Church fulfill the Great Commission: to make disciples of all men?

5 | conclude

- With your child, pray the Our Father.

6 | follow up

During the week, do at least one of the following activities with your child:
1. Memorize Mark 1:17.
2. Make a map of the missionary journeys of the Apostles in the early Church.
3. During your family's evening prayers, pray for Catholics around the world who face persecution for their Faith.

And Jesus said to them, "Follow me and I will make you become fishers of men."
—Mark 1:17

notes

_____

_____

_____

_____

_____

_____

_____

The Nature of the Church

Lesson Focus | To understand what the Church is, we first have to understand that she is Christ's Mystical Body. All her members are intimately united to him through Baptism, so what we do to others, we also do to Christ. The Church is one, holy, catholic, and apostolic. These are the four marks of the Church, and they establish that the Catholic Church is the Church Christ founded. He founded her to bring to all men the salvation he won for them. This happens through the Sacraments and the Church's teaching.

1 | begin

- Pray the Glory Be with your child.
- Show your child pictures of some things used as images for the Church: mustard seed, bride, body, sheep flock, vineyard, pearl, mother, etc.
- Read Matthew 13:31–33 and 13:44–48 aloud.

2 | summarize

Summarize this week's lesson for your child:

Example: *Jesus had to use many different images to describe the Church because the nature of the Church isn't something that can be summed up easily. If we want to understand the Church, we have to look at those images, the four marks, and her mission in the world.*

3 | review

Review this week's lesson by asking your child the following questions:

1. How is the Church a Mystical Body? (*Just as the head guides the other parts of the body, Christ guides us; we do Christ's work in the world; when we do good or harm to others, we are doing good or harm to Christ.*)
2. How is the Church one? (*The Church is one in unity, belief, worship, and liturgy under Christ.*)
3. How is the Church holy? (*The Church is holy in her divine origin and purpose and in her members who open themselves to grace.*)
4. How is the Church catholic? (*The Church has the fullness of Christ's truth for all peoples in all times.*)
5. How is the Church apostolic? (*She originated with the Apostles, professes the same doctrine as the Apostles, and continues to be led by the Apostles' successors.*)
6. Why is the Church necessary for our salvation? (*Because it is through her Sacraments that we receive sanctifying grace and are strengthened and confirmed in grace.*)

References

- Student Textbook: Chapter 3, pp. 19–24

- Sacred Scripture: Mk 4:30–32; Lk 8:5–12; Jn 10:1–10; 14:2; 1 Cor 3:9; 12:12–31; Eph 5:23–33

- *Catechism of the Catholic Church:* 751–57, 811–96

The disciples at Christ's Ascension.

4 | apply

Help your child apply this week's lesson by asking the following questions:

1. Why do you think the nature of the Church is so complex?
2. How do you think of the Church? Which of Christ's images makes the most sense to you?
3. What are some ways you can grow in your understanding of the Church?

5 | conclude

- With your child, pray the Our Father.

6 | follow up

During the week, do at least one of the following activities with your child:

1. Memorize Matthew 25:40.
2. Read Saint Paul's conversion story in Acts 9:1–30. Find online the painting of the event by Caravaggio, *The Conversion of Saint Paul*. Discuss how that event changed Paul and why.
3. Include a petition for unity among Christians in your family's evening prayers.

And the King will answer them, "Truly, I say to you, as you did it to one of the least of these my brethren, you did it to me."
—Matthew 25:40

notes

_____

_____

_____

_____

_____

_____

_____

The Teaching Church

Lesson Focus | So that we might know and love him better, God revealed himself to us through his dealings with Israel, through the words of the prophets, and finally and fully through the Incarnation of Jesus Christ. That revelation has been preserved through Sacred Scripture and Sacred Tradition. It has been taught, interpreted, and defended against errors by the Apostles, their successors, priests, and faithful Catholics. Through her creeds, her councils, her magisterial writings, and the writings of her great saints and doctors, the Church has handed on intact all that Christ taught and God revealed.

1 | begin

- Pray the Glory Be with your child.
- Visit the Vatican website: www.vatican.va. On the entry page click "English," then on the home page click "Encyclicals." Explain that these are papal writings that help Catholics understand and live the gospel in our time.
- Read 1 Timothy 6:20 aloud.

2 | summarize

Summarize this week's lesson for your child:

Example: *Guarding what has been entrusted to her is one of the most important parts of the Church's mission. She does that in many ways, including through her creeds, councils, the writings of holy and wise Catholics, and the writings of the Popes.*

3 | review

Review this week's lesson by asking your child the following questions:

1. Define *revelation*. (*Communication by God to humanity.*)
2. Who are the Apostolic Fathers? (*Christian teachers who were personally taught by the Apostles.*)
3. Define *magisterium*. (*The teaching body of the Church.*)
4. Define *ecumenical council*. (*A gathering of all the bishops, with the consent of the Pope, to discuss matters of concern to the Church.*)
5. Define *Doctors of the Church*. (*Holy teachers of Christian doctrine.*)
6. Define *Fathers of the Church*. (*Important early Christian writers.*)
7. Define *sensus fidei*. (*What Christ's followers have believed for centuries.*)
8. Can Christian doctrine change? (*No, but our understanding of it can deepen.*)

References

- Student Textbook: Chapter 4, pp. 25–31

- Sacred Scripture: Eph 1:4–5, 9; 2:18; 1 Tim 6:20; 2 Pet 1:4

- *Catechism of the Catholic Church*: 51–95, 101–27, 185–97, 884–92, 2033

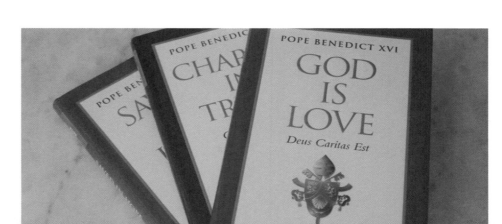

4 | apply

Help your child apply this week's lesson by asking the following questions:

1. What do you think would happen to the truths Christ entrusted to us without the Church to guard, hand on, and interpret them? Why would that be a problem?
2. Sometimes people struggle to accept others' authority. Why do you think this is?
3. What reasons do you have for trusting the Church's teaching authority? How do you think it will help you to continue to trust her as you grow older?

5 | conclude

- With your child, pray the Our Father.

6 | follow up

During the week, do at least one of the following activities with your child:

1. Memorize 1 Timothy 6:20.
2. Learn about Saint Athanasius and the persecution he faced in defending truth.
3. Write out Saint Teresa of Avila's Bookmark (see Appendix). Encourage your child to hang it where he will see it every day.

> *O Timothy, guard what has been entrusted to you. Avoid the godless chatter and contradictions of what is falsely called knowledge.*
> —1 Timothy 6:20

notes

_____

_____

_____

_____

_____

_____

_____

Authority in the Church—Teaching and Governing

Lesson Focus | So that his work on earth could continue, Christ commissioned his Apostles (and in turn their successors) to teach and govern his Church. To assist them in that work, the Holy Spirit gives the Pope, and the bishops in union with the Pope, the gift of infallibility. This means that, when certain conditions are met, the teachings of the Pope and ecumenical councils on faith and morals are free from error. The Pope and the bishops in union with him also have the authority to establish Church disciplines—rules that, unlike doctrine, can change with time.

1 | begin

- Pray the Glory Be with your child.
- Explain to your child the two types of rules in your home. First, rules that are universal and unchanging in all homes—no lying, hitting, etc. Second, rules particular to your home that help life run smoothly and can change—bedtimes, television privileges, etc.
- Read Matthew 18:15–18 aloud.

2 | summarize

Summarize this week's lesson for your child:

Example: *Jesus gave his Apostles authority to teach, define, and defend the unchanging universal teachings of his Church (called doctrines), as well as to establish rules that can change depending on the time, place, and needs of the Church (called disciplines).*

References

- Student Textbook: Chapter 5, pp. 32–38
- Sacred Scripture: Mt 18:15–18; Jn 8:32; 14:26
- *Catechism of the Catholic Church*: 42, 85–95, 832, 871–96, 1730–48, 2041–43

3 | review

Review this week's lesson by asking your child the following questions:

1. Define *infallibility*. (*Protection from teaching error in matters of faith and morals.*)
2. Who has the gift of infallibility? (*The Pope and the bishops teaching in union with him.*)
3. Is everything the Pope says infallible? (*No, he must be speaking to the whole Church and intending to use his authority to pronounce an unchangeable decision.*)
4. Is the Pope free from sin? (*No, infallibility only protects the Pope from error in certain teachings.*)
5. Can a Pope ever change a Church doctrine? What is an example of a doctrine? (*No; the Incarnation, Mary's perpetual virginity, the Blessed Trinity, the nature of marriage, the sanctity of life, etc.*)
6. Can a Pope change a discipline? What is an example of a discipline? (*Yes; the length of the fast before Mass, rules about fasting and abstinence, etc.*)

4 | apply

Help your child apply this week's lesson by asking the following questions:

1. How does knowing the truth about the moral law make you free? How are you more free than someone who doesn't know or obey any moral law?
2. If you were Jesus, why would you want to give the Pope the gift of infallibility?
3. How can you show your respect for the authority entrusted to the Church by Jesus?

5 | conclude

- With your child, pray the Our Father.

6 | follow up

During the week, do at least one of the following activities with your child:

1. Memorize John 8:32.
2. As a family, watch a movie about the life of Blessed John Paul II.
3. During family prayers, pray for the Pope and your bishop.

You will know the truth, and the truth will make you free.
—John 8:32

notes

_____

_____

_____

_____

_____

_____

_____

The Visible Hierarchical Church

Lesson Focus | The Church's governing structure is different from other governing structures in that it is supernatural. It was established by Christ, acts with his authority, and is guided by the Holy Spirit. The Pope is the visible head of the worldwide Church, bishops are the heads of the Church in their dioceses, and priests serve under them by helping govern individual parishes. Deacons assist priests in their work. The outlines of this structure were established by Christ and developed over time to meet the people's needs.

1 | begin

- Pray the Glory Be with your child.
- Tell your child a story about or a memory of your favorite priest.
- Read Acts 1:15–26 aloud.

2 | summarize

Summarize this week's lesson for your child:

Example: *Priests are part of the visible, hierarchical structure of the Church. Although the structure of the Church has grown and expanded as the Church has grown and expanded, it remains supernatural in its origins and follows the outlines of the structure Christ established.*

3 | review

Review this week's lesson by asking your child the following questions:

1. Define *diocese*. (*A portion of God's people united in faith and the Sacraments under the pastoral care of a bishop.*)
2. Define *bishop*. (*A successor of the Apostles who has received the fullness of the priesthood and is the spiritual leader of Catholics in his diocese.*)
3. Define *priest*. (*A man chosen by God to preach, to offer the Eucharistic sacrifice, to pray, and to guide God's people under the authority of a bishop.*)
4. Who is the vicar of Christ in the world? (*The Pope.*)
5. What are two honorary titles the Pope can give? (*Monsignor and Cardinal.*)
6. What is the name of the body of officials who assist bishops and Popes in governing a diocese or the universal Church? (*Curia.*)

References

- Student Textbook: Chapter 6, pp. 39–42
- Sacred Scripture: Acts 1:15–26
- *Catechism of the Catholic Church*: 77–79, 758–69, 833, 858–96, 1536–1600

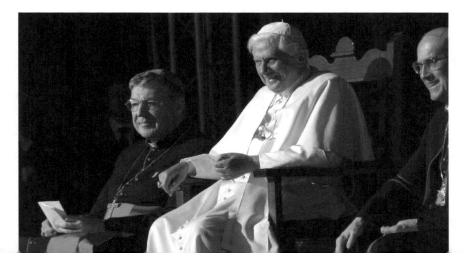

4 | apply

Help your child apply this week's lesson by asking the following questions:

1. How is the governing structure of the Church different from the governing structure of a country or a city?
2. What problems could arise if the Church's governing structure were like a city's governing structure?
3. How is the Church's governing structure more like the governing structure of a family? Why is that appropriate?

5 | conclude

- With your child, pray the Our Father.

6 | follow up

During the week, do at least one of the following activities with your child:

1. Memorize Ephesians 4:11.
2. If possible, attend Mass at your diocesan cathedral sometime in the next month.
3. Learn online about the election of Pope Saint Fabian and the Holy Spirit's role in the vote.

> *And his gifts were that some should be apostles, some prophets, some evangelists, some pastors and teachers.*
> —Ephesians 4:11

notes

_____

_____

_____

_____

_____

_____

_____

The Church Sanctifying—Sacraments of Membership

Lesson Focus | Through the Church, the grace won by Christ on the Cross is poured out into our souls. The Sacraments are the primary means by which we receive this grace. Of the seven Sacraments, three—Baptism, Eucharist, and Confirmation—are set apart as Sacraments of Initiation. By them, we receive new life in Christ, nourish that life, and are strengthened in it. All Catholics around the world and in all times have celebrated these Sacraments, although the manner in which they're celebrated differs among rites.

1 | begin

- Pray the Glory Be with your child.
- Show your child any pictures you have of your Baptism, First Communion, or Confirmation.
- Read John 3:1–6 aloud.

2 | summarize

Summarize this week's lesson for your child:

Example: *In the Sacraments of Initiation we are born anew. We receive new life in Baptism, nourish that life with the Eucharist, and strengthen it in Confirmation.*

3 | review

Review this week's lesson by asking your child the following questions:

1. What is the matter for each of the three Sacraments of Initiation? (*Baptism—water; Eucharist—bread and wine; Confirmation—laying on of the hands and anointing with sacred chrism.*)
2. Who is the minister of each of those Sacraments? (*Baptism—bishop, priest, or deacon; Eucharist—priest; Confirmation—bishop.*)
3. What are the words used for each? (*Baptism—"I baptize you in the name of the Father, and of the Son, and of the Holy Spirit; Eucharist—"This is my Body... This is the chalice of my Blood"; Confirmation—"Be sealed with the gift of the Holy Spirit."*)
4. Which of these Sacraments does not leave an indelible mark on the soul? (*Eucharist.*)
5. Which Sacrament calls us in a special way to be witnesses to the Faith? (*Confirmation.*)
6. Which Sacrament makes us brothers and sisters of Christ? (*Baptism.*)

References

- Student Textbook: Chapter 7, pp. 43–53
- Sacred Scripture: Mt 26:26–28; 28:18–20; Jn 3:5; 6:35–39; 20:22; Acts 2:1–11
- *Catechism of the Catholic Church:* 1203, 1212–74, 1285–1314, 1322–1405

4 | apply

Help your child apply this week's lesson by asking the following questions:
1. How can you protect the new life you received in Baptism?
2. How can you grow closer to Christ through the Eucharist?
3. What are some ways you can be a witness to the Faith every day?

5 | conclude

- With your child, pray the Our Father.

6 | follow up

During the week, do at least one of the following activities with your child:
1. Memorize John 3:5.
2. If possible, attend the Divine Liturgy at (or simply visit) an Eastern rite church in your area. Or search online for examples of Eastern rite sacred art and architecture.
3. Research the life of Saint Francis Xavier and the work he did to spread the gospel. Encourage your child to illustrate or dramatize key events, if possible.

> *Jesus answered, "Truly, truly, I say to you, unless one is born of water and the Spirit, he cannot enter the kingdom of God."*
> —John 3:5

notes

_____

_____

_____

_____

_____

_____

_____

The Church Sanctifying—Worship

Lesson Focus | God calls his children to worship him both privately (through prayer) and publicly (through liturgy). Our participation in the liturgy is essential. Through it, we give God the honor he is due, publicly attest to our Faith and how God blesses us, recognize that we are part of a family of believers, and receive the graces we need to grow in faith. The liturgy consists of the Mass, the Sacraments, and the Liturgy of the Hours. Changing liturgical seasons help us understand different dimensions of Christ and the Christian life.

1 | begin

- Pray the Glory Be with your child.
- Tell your child what your favorite liturgical season, feast day, or holy day is and why.
- Read Ephesians 3:7–21 aloud.

2 | summarize

Summarize this week's lesson for your child:

Example: *We must do more than pray to God; we also need to worship him. And we need to worship him with others, as part of a Christian family. We do this in the liturgy.*

3 | review

Review this week's lesson by asking your child the following questions:

1. What is liturgy? (*The Church's official public worship.*)
2. Name the three elements of Catholic liturgy? (*The Mass; the Sacraments; and the Divine Office, or Liturgy of the Hours.*)
3. What happens in each? (*In the Mass, we perfectly join with Christ's offering of himself to the Father and are nourished by the Eucharist; in the Sacraments, we receive God's grace and partake in the supernatural life; in the Divine Office we sanctify our day with prayer and join our prayers to the prayers of the whole Church.*)
4. What are the five liturgical colors, when are they used, and what does each symbolize? (*1. Green—ordinary time—life, hope; 2. Red—Pentecost, martyrs' feasts—fire, blood; 3. White—Christmas, Easter—joy, glory, purity; 4. Purple—Advent, Lent—penance, sorrow; 5. Rose—Gaudete and Laetare Sunday—joy in the midst of penance.*)

References

- Student Textbook: Chapter 8, pp. 54–60
- Sacred Scripture: Eph 1:9; 2:4; 3:9–17
- *Catechism of the Catholic Church*: 522–26, 540, 731–41, 1077–1109, 1163–78

4 | apply

Help your child apply this week's lesson by asking the following questions:

1. What does participating in the Church's liturgy give you that private prayer doesn't?
2. What would it say to people about our faith if we never worshipped God publicly?
3. What is your favorite feast day? What could we do to celebrate it this year?

5 | conclude

- With your child, pray the Our Father.

6 | follow up

During the week, do at least one of the following activities with your child:

1. Memorize Ephesians 2:4–5.
2. Purchase a subscription to *Magnificat* or buy a Breviary so your family can pray parts of the Divine Office together in the morning or evening. Or attend evening prayer at a nearby church, monastery, or convent.
3. As a family, attend a weekday or Saturday Mass in addition to Sunday Mass.

But God, who is rich in mercy, out of the great love with which he loved us, even when we were dead through our trespasses, made us alive together with Christ.
—Ephesians 2:4–5

notes

_____

_____

_____

_____

_____

_____

_____

Lesson 9

Mary—Mother of the Church

Lesson Focus | The Church refers to Mary as the New Eve, because through her yes she cooperated with Christ in redeeming man from sin and giving new life to the world. As such, she is "Mother of all the living," Christ's own Mother, and Mother of the Church. Because of her yes, God granted Mary special privileges, including her Immaculate Conception, perpetual virginity, and Assumption into Heaven. We too are called to grant her a special privilege by honoring her more than all the other saints and loving her as our own Mother.

1 | begin

- Pray the Glory Be with your child.
- Tell your child about your own relationship with Mary, a time you turned to her in need, a time she helped you, or what you've learned from her about following Christ.
- Read Luke 1:26–56 aloud.

2 | summarize

Summarize this week's lesson for your child:

Example: *Because Mary said yes to God, he could send Jesus into the world. For that reason, and for all the ways she loved Christ and now loves us, we honor her more than all the saints.*

3 | review

References

- Student Textbook: Chapter 9, pp. 61–67

- Sacred Scripture: Gen 3; Mt 1:18–24; Lk 1:26–56; Jn 2:1–11; 19:26–27

- *Catechism of the Catholic Church*: 148–49, 484–511, 963–71, 2617–19, 2705–8

Review this week's lesson by asking your child the following questions:

1. What was the Annunciation? (*The event in which Gabriel announced to Mary that she would be the Mother of God and she said yes.*)
2. What is *fiat*, and when was it said? (*"Let it be done" in Latin; at the Annunciation.*)
3. Define *Immaculate Conception*. (*Mary's conception in her mother's womb free from Original Sin.*)
4. Define *perpetual virginity*. (*Mary's being a virgin before, during, and after Jesus' birth.*)
5. Do Catholics worship Mary? (*No, we worship only God. We venerate Mary because of her role in our salvation and because Jesus asks us to honor and love her.*)
6. What doctrine teaches that Mary is in heaven with her body and soul? (*The Assumption.*)

4 | apply

Help your child apply this week's lesson by asking the following questions:

1. What is your favorite title for Mary? Why? What does it say about her?
2. What does Mary's example teach you about following Christ? How could you be a better imitator of Mary?
3. How often do you pray to Mary? Ask her for help? When else could you turn to her?

5 | conclude

- With your child, pray the Our Father.

6 | follow up

During the week, do at least one of the following activities with your child:

1. Memorize Luke 1:38a.
2. As a family, pray the Litany of Loreto (see Appendix).
3. Learn about Our Lady of Fatima and the miracle of the sun. Rent a movie about Fatima and watch it as a family.

> *And Mary said, "Behold, I am the handmaid of the Lord; let it be to me according to your word."*
> —Luke 1:38

notes

_____

_____

_____

_____

_____

_____

_____

Lesson 10

The Communion of Saints

Lesson Focus | The Communion of Saints includes all the faithful who are united in Christ: the Church Militant on earth, the Church Suffering in purgatory, and the Church Triumphant in heaven. By our prayers and sacrifices, we can help those who are part of the Church Suffering, and, by their prayers, those who are part of the Church Suffering and the Church Triumphant can help us here on earth. To honor a saint is to honor God, because the saint is his handiwork, a human person made holy by his grace.

1 | begin

- Pray the Glory Be with your child.
- Tell your child who your favorite saint is and why.
- Read Revelation 7:9–12 aloud.

2 | summarize

Summarize this week's lesson for your child:

Example: *The Church is so much bigger than the people we see at Mass on Sunday. All the souls in heaven and in purgatory, plus all those on earth who love and follow Christ, are part of the Church and are united in love for him.*

3 | review

Review this week's lesson by asking your child the following questions:

1. Define *Communion of Saints*. (*The relationship between the members of the Church in heaven, in purgatory, and on earth.*)
2. Define *canonized saint*. (*Someone the Church has officially declared to be in heaven.*)
3. What happens in purgatory? (*The soul is purified and made ready to see God.*)
4. Why is our intercession for the souls in purgatory important? (*They can't do anything to help themselves, so they rely on the help of the Church Militant and the Church Triumphant to intercede for them that they may enter heaven soon.*)
5. What does it mean to honor or venerate a saint? (*To pray to him and ask for his help, learn about him, and follow his example.*)
6. What is the Church Militant fighting? (*Temptation and sin.*)

References

- Student Textbook: Chapter 10, pp. 68–73
- Sacred Scripture: Mt 18:20; Rom 8:28; 15:25; 2 Cor 2:2; Eph 1:1; Phil 1:1; Col 1:2; Rev 7:9–12
- *Catechism of the Catholic Church*: 686–88, 946–62, 1030–32, 2156, 2634–36, 2683–84

216 | G8–10

4 | apply

Help your child apply this week's lesson by asking the following questions:
1. In what ways can your relationship with a saint be like your relationship with a friend?
2. What are some things you can do to help the souls in purgatory? Who do you know that has died and might be in need of our prayers?
3. Do you have a favorite saint? Who? Why?

5 | conclude

- With your child, pray the Our Father.

6 | follow up

During the week, do at least one of the following activities with your child:
1. Memorize Revelation 7:9–10.
2. Pay a visit to your church to light a candle and say a prayer for your deceased friends and relatives.
3. Choose a classic movie about a saint—*A Man for All Seasons*, *Joan of Arc*, *The Song of Bernadette*, *A Time for Miracles*, etc.—and watch it as a family.

After this I looked, and behold, a great multitude which no man could number, from every nation, from all tribes and peoples and tongues, standing before the throne and before the Lamb, clothed in white robes, with palm branches in their hands, and crying out with a loud voice, "Salvation belongs to our God who sits upon the throne, and to the Lamb!"
—Revelation 7:9–10

notes

_____
_____
_____
_____
_____
_____
_____
_____

Saints in Our History—The First Thousand Years

Lesson Focus | For two thousand years, the Church has endured, despite attacks from without and within. In the first several centuries, these attacks came primarily from without, as Christians were persecuted for their Faith. Later, they came from within, as some Christians spread false teachings about Christ and others lived lives that did not reflect the truth of the gospel. Despite all these attacks, however, God always raised up faithful believers to help strengthen the Church and defend her.

1 | begin

- Pray the Glory Be with your child.
- Talk to your child about the attacks the Church faces today—from the media, from the government, or from people who claim to be Catholic but publicly act against her.
- Read the story (or excerpts) of Saint Stephen's martyrdom in Acts 6—7 aloud.

2 | summarize

Summarize this week's lesson for your child:

Example: *For two thousand years, the Church has faced attacks from without and within. To defend her, many Catholics have given their lives. Saint Stephen was the first to do this.*

References

- Student Textbook: Chapter 11, pp. 74–79

- Sacred Scripture: Mt 28:19; Acts 2:1–4; 6:1—7:60

- *Catechism of the Catholic Church*: 77–79, 817, 914–16, 920–21, 2473–74

3 | review

Review this week's lesson by asking your child the following questions:

1. What is a Gentile? (*Someone who is not Jewish.*)
2. Define *martyr*. (*Someone who gives his life to defend, teach, or proclaim the Faith.*)
3. What is heresy? (*The obstinate denial of a basic teaching of the Catholic Faith.*)
4. What did the heresy of Arianism deny? (*Christ's divinity.*)
5. Identify the following people: Constantine (*Roman emperor who legalized Christianity*); Benedict (*Founder of Western Monasticism*); Peter (*First Pope*); Perpetua and Felicity (*Early Christian martyrs*); Paul (*Convert and Apostle to the Gentiles*); Augustine (*Convert, bishop, and theologian*); Arius (*Heretic who denied Christ's divinity*); Athanasius (*Opponent of Arianism*); Columban (*Irish missionary monk*).

4 | apply

Help your child apply this week's lesson by asking the following questions:

1. Why do you think someone would rather die than renounce his Faith?
2. For whom or for what would you give your life?
3. Of all the saints studied in this chapter, who is your favorite? How can you follow his example?

5 | conclude

- With your child, pray the Our Father.

6 | follow up

During the week, do at least one of the following activities with your child:

1. Memorize John 15:13.
2. Read more about one of the saints from this chapter. Dramatize their martyrdom.
3. Research the history of Saint Peter's tomb and its discovery during World War II.

> *Greater love has no man than this, that a man lay down his life for his friends.*
> —John 15:13

notes

_____

_____

_____

_____

_____

_____

_____

Saints in Our History—The Second Thousand Years

Lesson Focus | In many ways the challenges the Church faced in the second thousand years of her existence were the same as those she faced in the first thousand years. She faced persecution from without, losing the Holy Land to Muslims, and problems of corruption from within. There were likewise heresies to be dealt with that came from outside (modernism) and inside (leading up to the Reformation). But, as always, the Holy Spirit raised up great saints who helped Catholics know and live the truth.

1 | begin

- Pray the Glory Be with your child.
- Talk to your child about other threats the Church is under today— opposition to her teachings on marriage, family, and life; state attempts to silence her, etc.
- Read Matthew 7:13–27 aloud.

2 | summarize

Summarize this week's lesson for your child:

Example: *Christ warned us that people would try to mislead us and teach false things about him. But he also promised us that he would help us to combat those false teachings.*

References

- Student Textbook: Chapter 12, pp. 80–87

- Sacred Scripture: Mt 5:3; 19:24

- *Catechism of the Catholic Church*: 9, 849–56, 1897– 1904, 2108–9, 2123–28, 2244–46

3 | review

Review this week's lesson by asking your child the following questions:
1. What were the Crusades? (*The military efforts of Christians in the eleventh, twelfth, and thirteenth centuries to retake the Holy Land from Muslim control.*)
2. What was the Protestant Reformation? (*When many, in a misguided attempt to reform the Church, broke away from her.*)
3. What was the Counter-Reformation? (*The period of true reformation following the Council of Trent.*)
4. What is Modernism? (*The belief that faith and morals should evolve and that there is no unchanging revelation from God.*)
5. Identify the following: Saint Louis IX (*Holy king*); Saint Catherine of Siena (*Holy Italian laywoman*); Saint Elizabeth Ann Seton (*First American-born saint*); Martin Luther (*Leader of the Protestant Reformation*); Saint Francis Xavier (*Missionary to Asia*); Saint Francis of Assisi (*Founder of the Franciscans who preached reform and lived poverty*); Saint Maximillian Kolbe (*Franciscan who founded Knights of the Immaculata*); Saint Pius X (*Twentieth century Pope who combated modernism*); Saint Dominic (*Founder of the Order of Preachers*); Saint Ignatius (*Founder of the Society of Jesus—the Jesuits*).

4 | apply

Help your child apply this week's lesson by asking the following questions:

1. Why do you think the Church has faced so many attacks from those outside the Church?
2. Should we be surprised when Catholics, even her leaders, sin? Why or why not?
3. Who was your favorite saint who you studied in this chapter? What can you learn from him?

5 | conclude

- With your child, pray the Our Father.

6 | follow up

During the week, do at least one of the following activities with your child:

1. Memorize Matthew 7:13–14.
2. Learn more about one of the saints in this chapter. Write a story about his life.
3. If possible, go to Benediction. Explain that Saint Thomas Aquinas wrote the *Tantum Ergo*, which is usually sung at Benediction.

Enter by the narrow gate; for the gate is wide and the way is easy, that leads to destruction, and those who enter by it are many. For the gate is narrow and the way is hard, that leads to life, and those who find it are few.

—Matthew 7:13–14

notes

_____

_____

_____

_____

_____

_____

_____

Separated Brethren

Lesson Focus | The Catholic Church is the one true Church founded by Christ. In her are all the truths necessary for salvation. That doesn't mean, however, that those who aren't Catholic can't be saved. All Christians are our separated brethren and in communion with the Church, although that communion is imperfect. Others outside the Church can be saved, even though they have never met Christ, if they sincerely seek to serve God or would have if they knew him. Still, we should strive to bring all people to the fullness of faith.

1 | begin

- Pray the Glory Be with your child.
- Ask your child whom he knows who isn't Catholic. Of what religion, if any, is he?
- Read Matthew 19:16–22 aloud.

2 | summarize

Summarize this week's lesson for your child:

Example: *Like the man in the Scriptue passage, some people have a hard time accepting some or even all of Jesus' teachings. Others have never heard of Jesus or what he had to say. Our job, as Catholics, is to love all those people, respect them, and do what we can to bring them to the fullness of faith.*

3 | review

Review this week's lesson by asking your child the following questions:

1. Who are our separated brethren? (*Those who have been baptized but are not part of the visible Catholic Church, such as Protestant and Orthodox Christians, but who share some aspects of our Faith.*)
2. What is the difference between an atheist and an agnostic? (*An atheist denies God's existence. An agnostic thinks that God may exist, but that we can't know for certain.*)
3. What is our relationship with the Jews? (*God made the Jews the first chosen people; he revealed himself to the Jews; salvation came to us through the Jews.*)
4. What is our relationship with the Muslims? (*The Muslims believe in and worship one God, the Creator.*)
5. Why are animism and polytheism expressions of paganism? (*Both are forms of idolatry.*)
6. What is ecumenism? (*The effort to reunite all those outside the Church in the Mystical Body of Christ.*)
7. Why is ecumenism important for salvation? (*The Church is the ordinary means by which salvation comes and contains all that is necessary for our salvation.*)

References

- Student Textbook: Chapter 13, pp. 88–94
- Sacred Scripture: Mt 19:16–22; Jn 6:66; Acts 11
- *Catechism of the Catholic Church:* 817–22, 838–48, 1258–60, 2112, 2123–28

4 | apply

Help your child apply this week's lesson by asking the following questions:

1. Why should you want to share the fullness of your Faith with others?
2. What are three ways you can share the Catholic Faith with those outside the Church?
3. What should you not say or do when sharing the Faith with others?

5 | conclude

- With your child, pray the Our Father.

6 | follow up

During the week, do at least one of the following activities with your child:

1. Memorize 1 Peter 3:15.
2. As a family, pray for those you love who have left the Church or don't know Christ.
3. Invite a non-Catholic friend to a youth group event, Mass, or retreat.

> *Always be prepared to make a defense to any one who calls you to account for the hope that is in you, yet do it with gentleness and reverence.*
> —1 Peter 3:15

notes

_____

_____

_____

_____

_____

_____

_____

The Universal Call to Holiness

Lesson Focus | God calls each and every person to holiness. Part of answering that call is doing the work, or apostolate, God has for us. To become holy and carry out our work, we must overcome the obstacles that prevent us from doing his will. Primary among those obstacles are vices—sinful habits. There are seven capital sins: pride, avarice (covetousness), lust, anger, gluttony, envy, and sloth.

1 | begin

- Pray the Glory Be with your child.
- Tell your child about a vice against which you have struggled and (mostly) overcome. Explain how you have done that and what difference it has made to you and others.
- Read Matthew 5:48 aloud.

2 | summarize

Summarize this week's lesson for your child:

Example: *It seems as if Jesus asks a lot of us, but he always gives us the grace to do as he asks. Overcoming sin is no different. If we work hard to root out vice, Jesus will give us the help we need.*

3 | review

Review this week's lesson by asking your child the following questions:

1. What is the universal call to holiness? (*The call of each Christian to follow Christ so we may be with him in Heaven for eternity.*)
2. Define *apostolate*. (*The work of spreading the gospel in whatever way we can.*)
3. Define *capital sins*. (*The seven sins that are the source of all other vices and sins.*)
4. List and define the seven capital sins. (*Pride: excessive, disordered self love; covetousness: uncontrolled desire for possessions; lust: uncontrolled desire or indulgence in sexual pleasure; anger: uncontrolled expression of displeasure; gluttony: uncontrolled desire for and indulgence in food and drink; envy: unhappiness over the good fortune of others; sloth: excessive laziness, a lack of desire.*)

References

- Student Textbook: Chapter 14, pp. 96–101
- Sacred Scripture: Mt 25:14–27; 28:18–20; Gal 5:13–26; Eph 6:10–18; Col 4:2; 1 Pet 1:13–16
- *Catechism of the Catholic Church*: 1865–69, 1763–65, 2012–16, 2094, 2514–17, 2538–40

4 | apply

Help your child apply this week's lesson by asking the following questions:

1. For each of the seven capital sins, give one example of a sinful action that stems from that capital sin (e.g., covetousness: stealing).
2. What vice or vices do you struggle with in particular?
3. What are some things you can do to overcome that vice?

5 | conclude

- With your child, pray the Our Father.

6 | follow up

During the week, do at least one of the following activities with your child:

1. Memorize Matthew 5:48.
2. Pray the Prayer to Saint Michael (see Appendix) every night and ask for his help in fighting temptation.
3. Learn about Saint Josémaría Escrivá and how he believed we could grow in holiness through our work and daily lives.

> *You, therefore, must be perfect, as your heavenly Father is perfect.*
> —Matthew 5:48

notes

_____

_____

_____

_____

_____

_____

_____

The Life of Virtue

Lesson Focus | While vices are bad habits that get in the way of holiness, virtues are good habits that help us pursue holiness. There are three virtues we receive by grace: faith, hope, and love. We call these supernatural virtues. Other virtues are natural virtues, and we cultivate these through prayer and effort. There are four cardinal virtues—virtues upon which the exercise of other virtues hinges (prudence, justice, temperance, fortitude), and seven moral virtues that help us overcome the seven cardinal vices, or capital sins (humility, liberality, chastity, meekness, moderation, brotherly love, diligence.)

1 | begin

- Pray the Glory Be with your child.
- Tell your child how practicing a particular virtue has helped you live a more joyful life.
- Read 2 Peter 1:5–7 aloud.

2 | summarize

Summarize this week's lesson for your child:

Example: *Virtues are good habits that help us pursue holiness. The more we grow in virtue, the easier it becomes to do God's will. It also becomes easier to be joyful, grateful, and loving.*

3 | review

Review this week's lesson by asking your child the following questions:

1. What are the cardinal virtues? (*The chief moral virtues upon which the other virtues depend: prudence, justice, temperance, and fortitude.*)
2. Explain each of the four cardinal virtues. (*Prudence: helps us act and choose wisely; justice: helps us give God and our neighbor their due; temperance: helps us moderate our passions and desires; fortitude: helps us confront difficulties with courage.*)
3. What are moral virtues? (*Good habits acquired by repeatedly doing good: humility, liberality, chastity, meekness, moderation, brotherly love, and diligence.*)
4. What are theological virtues? (*The supernatural virtues that are given to us by God: faith, hope, and charity.*)
5. Explain each of the theological virtues. (*Faith: helps us believe in God; hope: helps us trust in God; charity: helps us love God and our neighbor.*)

References

- Student Textbook: Chapter 15, pp. 102–9

- Sacred Scripture: Lk 10:25–28

- *Catechism of the Catholic Church*: 1804–29, 2086–87, 2656–58

4 | apply

Help your child apply this week's lesson by asking the following questions:

1. What is an example of prudence? Justice? Fortitude? Temperance?
2. What is an action the virtue of faith makes possible? What about hope? Charity?
3. Which of the moral virtues can help you overcome the primary vices with which you struggle? What are some ways you can develop these virtues?

5 | conclude

- With your child, pray the Our Father.

6 | follow up

During the week, do at least one of the following activities with your child:

1. Memorize 2 Peter 1:5–7.
2. Remind your child to ask his guardian angel every day for help in growing in virtue.
3. Based upon your child's answer to question 3 in Step 4, help him pick three actions he can do in the next week to grow in a particular virtue.

For this very reason make every effort to supplement your faith with virtue, and virtue with knowledge, and knowledge with self-control, and self-control with steadfastness, and steadfastness with godliness, and godliness with brotherly affection, and brotherly affection with love.
—2 Peter 1:5–7

notes

_____

_____

_____

_____

_____

_____

_____

The Works of Mercy and Happiness

Lesson Focus | Christ promises those who follow him and do his will a happiness that is far more real and lasting than the happiness the world promises us through the pursuit of wealth, fame, and power. To attain that happiness, we must practice the Spiritual and Corporal Works of Mercy. We must also strive both to make our love for Christ and our neighbor the reason for doing those Works of Mercy and to perform the acts with love.

1 | begin

- Pray the Glory Be with your child.
- Tell your child about a time someone performed a Work of Mercy—Spiritual or Corporal—for you or your family. Why was it needed? How did it help you?
- Read Matthew 5:3–12 aloud.

2 | summarize

Summarize this week's lesson for your child:

Example: *If we want to be truly happy, we must seek to love people as God asks us to, caring for both their bodies and souls through the Spiritual and Corporal Works of Mercy.*

3 | review

Review this week's lesson by asking your child the following questions:

1. What does Jesus promise to those who accept his teaching and follow his example? (*Happiness in the next life and true peace and joy in this life.*)
2. What are the seven Spiritual Works of Mercy? (*Admonish the sinner; instruct the ignorant; counsel the doubtful; comfort the sorrowful; bear wrongs patiently; forgive all injuries; pray for the living and the dead.*)
3. What are the seven Corporal Works of Mercy? (*Feed the hungry; give drink to the thirsty; clothe the naked; visit the imprisoned; shelter the homeless; visit the sick; bury the dead.*)
4. What attitude should be at the heart of all our good works? (*Love.*)

References

- Student Textbook: Chapter 16, pp. 110–14
- Sacred Scripture: Mt 5—7, 25:31–46
- *Catechism of the Catholic Church*: 1716–24, 1822–29, 2443–49

4 | apply

Help your child apply this week's lesson by asking the following questions:

1. Can you give me an example of each of the seven Spiritual Works of Mercy?
2. Can you give me an example of each of the seven Corporal Works of Mercy?
3. Why do you think practicing the Works of Mercy leads to happiness? Why would failing to practice them lead to unhappiness?

5 | conclude

- With your child, pray the Our Father.

6 | follow up

During the week, do at least one of the following activities with your child:

1. Memorize Matthew 25:40.
2. As a family, pick one Corporal Work of Mercy you can do this week: collect no-longer-used clothes for the homeless; invite a new family in your parish to dinner; visit an elderly neighbor, etc.
3. Make or update a list of special prayer intentions. Is there someone you should be praying for but aren't? Write down your intentions, and pray for them nightly.

And the King will answer them, "Truly, I say to you, as you did it to one of the least of these my brethren, you did it to me."
—Matthew 25:40

notes

_____

_____

_____

_____

_____

_____

_____

The Religious Life and the Priesthood

Lesson Focus | God calls all his children to grow closer to him through making a gift of their lives to someone. Most people give their lives to another person in marriage. But some people receive a call to give their lives to God as priests and consecrated religious. Priests serve Christ by serving his Church. Religious sisters and brothers serve him through living lives devoted to prayer and service. Answering these calls requires tremendous generosity—the willingness to lay down their lives for God. Both, however, bring great rewards.

1 | begin

- Pray the Glory Be with your child.
- Tell your child about a faithful priest or religious brother or sister you've known. What did you like best about him or her? How did that person model Christ to you?
- Read John 21:15–19 aloud.

2 | summarize

Summarize this week's lesson for your child:

Example: *Just as Peter received a special call from God to serve him as Pope, other men and women receive a special call to serve him as priests and religious.*

3 | review

Review this week's lesson by asking your child the following questions:

1. Define *religious*. (*Those whose vocation is to follow Christ most perfectly on earth.*)
2. Define *clergy*. (*Ordained ministers—bishops, priests, deacons.*)
3. Define *vows*. (*Free, deliberate promises made to God.*)
4. What are the three evangelical counsels? (*Poverty—offering up the good of money and possessions; chastity—offering up the good of marriage and physical intimacy with one's spouse; and obedience—offering up the good of independence and freedom.*)
5. Do priests make the same vows as religious? (*No, they do not take a vow of poverty.*)
6. What is the difference between active and contemplative religious? (*Active religious serve God in the world as nurses, teachers, etc; contemplatives serve God through a life of prayer.*)

References

- Student Textbook: Chapter 17, pp. 115–20

- Sacred Scripture: Mt 19:10–12; 19:16–30; Lk 22:42

- *Catechism of the Catholic Church*: 782–86, 871–96, 914–33, 1536–1600

4 | apply

Help your child apply this week's lesson by asking the following questions:

1. How can taking a vow of poverty help someone serve God better? What about chastity? Obedience?
2. Do you think it's easier for lay people or for priests and religious to live holy lives? Why?
3. Do you think God is calling you to religious life (girl/boy) or to the priesthood (boy)?

5 | conclude

- With your child, pray the Our Father.

6 | follow up

During the week, do at least one of the following activities with your child:

1. Memorize John 15:1.
2. Pay a visit to a nearby convent or monastery. Call ahead to make arrangements and find out what time they offer Mass or pray the Liturgy of the Hours so you can join them.
3. During evening prayers, encourage your child to ask God to help him know his vocation and to give him the grace to pursue it.

I am the true vine, and my Father is the vinedresser.
—John 15:1

notes

_____

_____

_____

_____

_____

_____

_____

The Lay Apostolate

Lesson Focus | Those who don't enter the priesthood or religious life are the laity. Like priests and religious, lay people are called to serve God and others. They live that call, however, in the world, using the gifts that God gives them to bring the gospel into the culture. Their task is an important one, as their lives take them places that priests and religious rarely go. They must be careful, however, to be in the world, not of the world.

1 | begin

- Pray the Glory Be with your child.
- Give your child several examples of how you or other lay people in your parish serve God (e.g., teaching CCD, volunteering at crisis pregnancy centers, giving to the poor, etc.).
- Read Genesis 1:26–31 aloud.

2 | summarize

Summarize this week's lesson for your child:

Example: *Lay people have a very important job to do for God. He asks us to serve the Church and others in the world by bringing the gospel into our culture and our homes.*

3 | review

Review this week's lesson by asking your child the following questions:

1. Who are the laity? (*Baptized members of the Church who don't receive Holy Orders or enter a religious order.*)
2. How do the laity grow in holiness? (*By uniting themselves to Christ; through prayer, work, and the Sacraments; by serving the Church; and by being witnesses to Christ.*)
3. What three goods do the evangelical counsels ask religious to give up? (*Money, marriage, and freedom.*)
4. How are the laity called to use those goods to serve the Church? (*Support the Church and those in need; raise Catholic families; use their freedom to make Christ present everywhere in the world.*)

References

- Student Textbook: Chapter 18, pp. 121–23
- Sacred Scripture: Gen 1—2
- *Catechism of the Catholic Church*: 782–86, 873–75, 897–913, 2012–16, 2021–24

4 | apply

Help your child apply this week's lesson by asking the following questions:

1. As lay people, how can we sanctify the world through what we do in our home? In your classroom? In sports? At a party? With a friend?
2. Can you give me an example of a time you've helped bring the gospel into the world?
3. Why is it so important that lay people bring the gospel into the world? Why can't we just leave that work to priests and religious?

5 | conclude

- With your child, pray the Our Father.

6 | follow up

During the week, do at least one of the following activities with your child:

1. Memorize Mark 16:15.
2. As a family, pray Blessed John Paul II's Prayer for the Laity (see Appendix).
3. Help your child purchase a necklace or T-shirt that is explicitly religious. Tell him that whenever he wears it, he should remember that he's witnessing to the gospel.

> *And he said to them, "Go into all the world and preach the gospel to the whole creation."*
> —Mark 16:15

notes

_____

_____

_____

_____

_____

_____

_____

_____

Marriage and the Family

Lesson Focus | God calls most men and women to make a gift of themselves, in love, through marriage. Marriage is the permanent union of one man and one woman. Through it two people give each other help and support in this life, bring new life into the world, and help each other grow in holiness so that they can reach heaven. Married couples are called to love each other and be faithful, raising and educating children in the Faith. In turn, children are called to love and honor their parents all their lives.

1 | begin

- Pray the Glory Be with your child.
- Show your child pictures from your wedding day (or a good friend's wedding day). Share some of your favorite memories from that day.
- Read Genesis 1:28 aloud.

2 | summarize

Summarize this week's lesson for your child:

Example: *From the very beginning, God has called men and women to give themselves to one another in love for the purpose of creating new life and so that couples can help each other in their daily tasks and quest for holiness.*

3 | review

Review this week's lesson by asking your child the following questions:

1. Define *conjugal love*. (*The total self-giving of man and woman as expressed in bodily union in the vocation of marriage.*)
2. Define *indissolubility*. (*The permanence of the union of husband and wife, which ends only with death.*)
3. Define *mutual sanctification*. (*The process of spouses becoming holy through their marriage; they help one another get to heaven.*)
4. What are the duties of parents? (*To be open to the gift of life, care for their children's bodily and spiritual needs, educate their children for this life and the next.*)
5. What are the duties of children? (*To obey their parents, show them respect and gratitude, and care for them in their old age.*)
6. What are the duties of husband and wife to one another? (*Support one another in life, help one another in their tasks on earth, help one another raise their children, sacrifice their individual freedom for the greater good.*)

References

- Student Textbook: Chapter 19, pp. 124–28
- Sacred Scripture: Gen 1:28; 2:18–24; Mt 19:6, 9; Jn 2:1–11
- *Catechism of the Catholic Church*: 369–73, 1601–58, 2201–31, 2335, 2360–79

4 | apply

Help your child apply this week's lesson by asking the following questions:

1. Why is it a lie when a couple has a physical relationship outside of marriage?
2. What are some of the threats to marriage and family that you see today?
3. How can you stand up against those threats?

5 | conclude

- With your child, pray the Our Father.

6 | follow up

During the week, do at least one of the following activities with your child:

1. Memorize Genesis 1:28.
2. Learn more about Saint Gianna Beretta Molla and why she is an important saint for today.
3. Find online a novena to Saint Joseph, and pray it for all the married couples and families you know.

And God blessed them, and God said to them, "Be fruitful and multiply, and fill the earth and subdue it; and have dominion over the fish of the sea and over the birds of the air and over every living thing that moves upon the earth."
—Genesis 1:28

notes

_____

_____

_____

_____

_____

_____

Lesson 20

The Christian in the World

Lesson Focus | As Christians, we belong to a community bigger than our family or parish. We also are part of civil society and have an obligation to work through society for the common good. Although we must not obey or support unjust laws, we are duty bound to pay taxes, defend our nation against aggressors, and support laws that are in conformity with God's laws. We also are called to exercise good stewardship over creation.

1 | begin

- Pray the Glory Be with your child.
- With your child, look at a newspaper or an online news magazine. Find stories of Catholics advocating for a specific issue or cause.
- Read Matthew 22:15–21 aloud.

2 | summarize

Summarize this week's lesson for your child:

Example: *As Jesus taught, Christians have duties to both the state (our country) and God. In fact, fulfilling our duties to the state is part of fulfilling our duty to God, who calls us to work in society for the common good.*

3 | review

Review this week's lesson by asking your child the following questions:

1. Define *common good*. (*The welfare of the whole community and not just one person.*)
2. Define *stewardship*. (*Caring for creation and using God's gifts wisely.*)
3. Define *patriotism*. (*Love of one's country.*)
4. Define *nationalism*. (*Disordered love of one's country in which one is blind to its defects.*)
5. What duties do Christians have to society? (*Pray for their country, serve others, obey just laws, pay taxes, work to help the less fortunate.*)
6. What good should a society do? (*Promote virtue, foster right values, and establish the conditions necessary for the proper exercise of freedom.*)

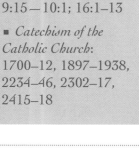

References

- Student Textbook: Chapter 20, pp. 129–33

- Sacred Scripture: Gen 1–2; 1 Sam 9:15 – 10:1; 16:1–13

- *Catechism of the Catholic Church*: 1700–12, 1897–1938, 2234–46, 2302–17, 2415–18

4 | apply

Help your child apply this week's lesson by asking the following questions:

1. What are two ways the government today fosters virtue?
2. What are some examples of ways the government undermines virtue or freedom?
3. Even though you can't vote yet, how can you still be a good citizen? What can you do to defend human dignity, the family, or religious freedom?

5 | conclude

- With your child, pray the Our Father.

6 | follow up

During the week, do at least one of the following activities with your child:

1. Memorize Matthew 22:21b.
2. During evening prayers, ask God to give the president, your congressman, and senators wisdom and love as they lead the country.
3. As a family, spend an hour on Saturday praying outside of an abortion clinic, contribute money to a crisis pregnancy center, or write to an elected official who supports an unjust law, such as abortion, same-sex marriage, or policies that hurt the family and urge him to change his position.

> *Render therefore to Caesar the things that are Caesar's, and to God the things that are God's.*
> —Matthew 22:21b

notes

_____

_____

_____

_____

_____

_____

_____

Law and Conscience

Lesson Focus | There are many kinds of laws. There are laws of nature, such as gravity. There are moral laws, such as the imperative not to murder. There are revealed laws made known to us by God, such as the command to love our neighbor as ourselves. There are also ecclesiastical laws (laws made by the Church) and civil laws (laws made by the government). Civil laws must not contradict moral laws, and moral and revealed laws can never change. We must form our conscience in accord with the moral law and the Church.

1 | begin

- Pray the Glory Be with your child.
- Drop a small ball, and ask your child what law makes it fall. Explain that nothing can change the law of gravity. Then explain that the same is true for other laws, such as moral laws. They always remain true, even if people break them.
- Read Romans 2:15 aloud.

2 | summarize

Summarize this week's lesson for your child:

Example: *There are many types of laws in the world. We need to understand them and know the differences between them, so we can form our consciences rightly and do good.*

References

- Student Textbook: Chapter 21, pp. 134–39

- Sacred Scripture: Mt 6:25–33; Lk 12:4–7; Rom 2:15

- *Catechism of the Catholic Church:* 574–82, 707–10, 1776–1800, 1950–74, 2041–43

3 | review

Review this week's lesson by asking your child the following questions:

1. What are moral laws? (*Laws that direct our wills toward the good and are unchanging.*)
2. What are civil laws? (*Laws made by civil or government authorities.*)
3. What is the natural law? (*The basic moral law placed in our hearts by God and knowable through the use of reason.*)
4. Who gives us revealed laws? (*God.*)
5. What are ecclesiastical laws? Can they be changed? (*Laws made by Church officials; yes.*)
6. What is a conscience, and how should it be formed? (*Our God-given internal guide that helps us distinguish right actions from wrong ones. We form it by looking to the Church for guidance and growing in knowledge and understanding of her teaching.*)
7. Can a well-formed conscience ever lead us to violate the Church's teachings? (*No.*)

4 | apply

Help your child apply this week's lesson by asking the following questions:
1. What are three things you can do to form your conscience correctly?
2. Why do you think God gives us the freedom to disobey moral laws?
3. What are some examples of choices that a poorly formed conscience could lead us to make?

5 | conclude

- With your child, pray the Our Father.

6 | follow up

During the week, do at least one of the following activities with your child:
1. Memorize Romans 2:15.
2. Search for Catholic websites where you can look for answers about the Faith (e.g., Catholics United for the Faith, Catholic Answers, the Saint Paul Center, etc.).
3. Read the words to Blessed John Henry Newman's hymn "Lead, Kindly Light," which can be found online. Learn about Newman and the circumstances that led him to write the hymn.

They show that what the law requires is written on their hearts, while their conscience also bears witness and their conflicting thoughts accuse or perhaps excuse them.
—Romans 2:15

notes

Lesson 22

The Church and the Social Order

Lesson Focus | The Church has a duty to do more than proclaim Christ. She also has a responsibility to shape society according to what is good and true. Although the Church leaves much to the prudential judgment of lawmakers, she also insists that certain principles should guide their decisions: a commitment to the protection of all life, a respect for marriage and family life, care for the poor, and just treatment of workers, as well as respect for freedom of conscience, belief, and private property.

1 | begin

- Pray the Glory Be with your child.
- Ask your child what he would do if he saw a friend doing something that would hurt himself very badly? Would he stand by and watch, or would he speak up?
- Read Matthew 28:19–20 aloud.

2 | summarize

Summarize this week's lesson for your child:

Example: *When we work to promote just laws in the world, we are answering the Great Commission. We're creating a culture of life, a culture that helps people to be happy and holy and not harm themselves.*

3 | review

Review this week's lesson by asking your child the following questions:

1. Who is hurt when the poor are oppressed? (*Everyone in society.*)
2. How is the family undermined when workers aren't paid a just wage? (*Families aren't able to support themselves, and they are put in difficult circumstances, often being forced to rely on others.*)
3. What harm comes from abortion? (*Innocent lives are taken, families are destroyed, women are hurt, motherhood is devalued, and the dignity of all life is undermined.*)
4. Can war ever be just? (*Yes, if a nation needs to defend itself and all other avenues of resolution have been tried and failed.*)
5. Is killing someone in self-defense murder? (*No, murder is the unjust taking of an innocent life.*)
6. Can abortion ever be good? (*No, taking an innocent life is always wrong.*)

References

- Student Textbook: Chapter 22, pp. 140–44

- Sacred Scripture: Gen 4:19; 18:20; 19:1–23; Ex 3:7–10; Deut 24:14–15; Mt 28:19–20; Jas 5:4

- *Catechism of the Catholic Church*: 1700–12, 1929–33, 2258–2330, 2419–49

A service for aborted babies.

4 | apply

Help your child apply this week's lesson by asking the following questions:

1. What is an injustice in our society today? How can we help stop that injustice?
2. If Christians never worked to build a better society, would we be failing to love our fellow man? Why or why not?
3. Why do you think some people don't speak up in the face of injustice? What stops them?

5 | conclude

- With your child, pray the Our Father.

6 | follow up

During the week, do at least one of the following activities with your child:

1. Memorize John 3:17.
2. Watch the film *Amazing Grace* to learn more about William Wilberforce and how he outlawed the slave trade in England.
3. Purchase a pro-life, pro-family bumper sticker for your family car.

For God sent the Son into the world, not to condemn the world, but that the world might be saved through him.
—John 3:17

notes

_____
_____
_____
_____
_____
_____
_____

Prayer

Lesson Focus | One of the pillars of Christian life is prayer. Just as no human relationship could grow or flourish without conversation, neither can our relationship with God flourish without prayer. At its heart, prayer is simply talking to God. We can pray by talking aloud, repeating memorized prayers, praying silently, or meditating upon him. When we pray, we should thank God for his good gifts, praise him for his goodness, ask for his forgiveness, and bring before him petitions for our needs.

1 | begin

- Pray the Glory Be with your child.
- Tell your child what your favorite prayer is and why.
- Read Matthew 6:8–15 aloud.

2 | summarize

Summarize this week's lesson for your child:

Example: *Jesus taught us to see God as our Father and to go to him with all our needs. God wants us to talk to him all the time about all things. That's what prayer is.*

3 | review

Review this week's lesson by asking your child the following questions:

1. What is prayer? (*The lifting of the heart and mind to God to know him better, adore him, thank him, and ask him for what we need.*)
2. What are the two kinds of prayer? (*Mental prayer and vocal prayer.*)
3. What are the five steps to prayer? (*To prepare ourselves, humble ourselves, have faith and confidence, resign ourselves to God's will, and persevere.*)
4. What is the difference between formal and informal prayer? (*Formal prayer follows a set pattern, while informal prayer is spontaneously talking to God in our own words.*)
5. What are the four reasons for prayer? (*Adoration, thanksgiving, contrition, petition.*)
6. What is liturgy? (*The Church's official public worship.*)

References

- Student Textbook: Chapter 23, pp. 146–51

- Sacred Scripture: Mt 6:8–15; 14:23; 19:13; 26:36–46; Lk 11:9–13; 18:1–8; Jn 14:16

- *Catechism of the Catholic Church*: 1174–78, 2598–2865

4 | apply

Help your child apply this week's lesson by asking the following questions:

1. What is your favorite prayer? Why?
2. How often do you talk to God as you go about your day? What do you talk about? What else could you talk about?
3. What is your biggest struggle with prayer? What are some ways to overcome it?

5 | conclude

- With your child, pray the Our Father.

6 | follow up

During the week, do at least one of the following activities with your child:

1. Memorize Luke 18:1.
2. Drop your child off at your church for a little prayer time while you run errands.
3. As a family, evaluate your prayer life. Are you praying together regularly? Why or why not? What changes could you make that could help you pray more?

And he told them a parable, to the effect that they ought always to pray and not lose heart.
—Luke 18:1

notes

_____

_____

_____

_____

_____

_____

_____

The Sacramental Life

Lesson Focus | To help us grow in holiness, Christ has given us the Sacraments, which make us holy by giving us grace, restoring us to grace, or increasing the life of grace within us. They are outward signs of an inward reality. They are also efficacious signs; this means that they make happen the very things they signify. Although all of the Sacraments are important in our journey toward holiness, the Sacraments of Penance and the Eucharist are especially important. They are like our "lifelines" to grace.

1 | begin

- Pray the Glory Be with your child.
- Tell your child why you love receiving the Eucharist or the Sacrament of Penance. How does it help you to be a better spouse, parent, friend, etc?
- Read John 20:19–23 aloud.

2 | summarize

Summarize this week's lesson for your child:

Example: *Before he ascended into heaven, Jesus gave his Apostles and their successors the power to celebrate the Sacraments. Through the Sacraments we become more like Christ.*

3 | review

Review this week's lesson by asking your child the following questions:

1. Why do we confess our sins to a priest? (*Because Christ gave the Apostles and their successors the authority to forgive sins.*)
2. What is contrition? (*Sorrow for our sins.*)
3. Why is the Eucharist the source and summit of the Christian life? (*Because it is both a means of receiving grace and the source of grace, Jesus himself.*)
4. How do we worthily receive Communion? (*Be in a state of grace, believe Jesus is truly present in the Sacrament, observe the fast, and spend time in thanksgiving.*)
5. What is transubstantiation? (*The changing of the bread and wine into the Body, Blood, Soul, and Divinity of Jesus, which occurs in the Consecration.*)

References

- Student Textbook: Chapter 24, pp. 152–59

- Sacred Scripture: Mt 26:26–28; 28:18–20; Jn 20:19–23; Eph 5:25–32; Heb 5:1–10; Jas 5:12–16

- *Catechism of the Catholic Church*: 1127–29, 1213–84, 1322–1498, 1996–2005, 2839–45

4 | apply

Help your child apply this week's lesson by asking the following questions:
1. How do you think the Sacraments have brought you closer to Christ?
2. Do you always receive the Eucharist as reverently and consciously as you should? Is there anything you could do to prepare yourself better for Communion?
3. How do you think Christ shows his love for you through the Sacraments? How can you show your love for him in return?

5 | conclude

- With your child, pray the Our Father.

6 | follow up

During the week, do at least one of the following activities with your child:
1. Memorize John 19:34.
2. As a family, go to confession this week.
3. Attend Mass on at least one extra day this week, or spend some quiet time in prayer with your child in front of the Blessed Sacrament.

> *But one of the soldiers pierced his side with a spear, and at once there came out blood and water.*
> —John 19:34

notes

_____
_____
_____
_____
_____
_____
_____
_____

Death and the Particular Judgment

Lesson Focus | The way we live our lives every day helps prepare us for meeting Jesus at the hour of our death, when our soul will be separated from our body. As soon as we die, we will meet Jesus, and he will make known to us the measure of good and evil in us. The closer we are to him in this life and the more we strive to love him and others, the less we'll fear that judgment and the more we'll be filled with joy at the thought of being with him.

1 | begin

- Pray the Glory Be with your child.
- Ask your child how he prepares for a test, a big game, a recital, or a school play.
- Read Sirach 1:11 aloud.

2 | summarize

Summarize this week's lesson for your child:

Example: *The more we follow God's will in this life, the more peaceful our death will be, for the greater will be our hope that we will spend a happy eternity with Christ.*

3 | review

Review this week's lesson by asking your child the following questions:

1. What is the Particular Judgment? (*The judgment every person will face at death, when the Lord will judge us on all we did and did not do and we will see ourselves as we truly are.*)
2. What is heaven? (*Eternal life and the enjoyment of the vision of God.*)
3. What is hell? (*Eternal suffering of separation from God.*)
4. What is purgatory? (*A state after death of temporary suffering that cleanses the soul and makes it worthy to see God.*)
5. What help does the Church offer us before we die? (*The Sacrament of the Anointing of the Sick, as well as confession and the Eucharist.*)
6. What is the Christian understanding of death? (*Death is not the end of life but the beginning of our eternal life with God. It is a transition to a new and eternal life.*)

References

- Student Textbook: Chapter 25, pp. 162–67

- Sacred Scripture: Gen 3; Sir 1:11; Mt 4:12–17; 16:18; 19:16–21; Jn 3:15–16; 5:24; Heb 9:27

- *Catechism of the Catholic Church*: 362–68, 400–3, 1005–14, 1021–37

4 | apply

Help your child apply this week's lesson by asking the following questions:
1. What are some things you can do every day to prepare your soul to meet Jesus?
2. What type of person do you want to be when you die? What do you need to do now to become that person?
3. What are some ways you can help the souls in Purgatory?

5 | conclude

- With your child, pray the Our Father.

6 | follow up

During the week, do at least one of the following activities with your child:
1. Memorize Sirach 1:11.
2. Visit the grave of a deceased loved one and say a prayer for him there.
3. Arrange to have a Mass said for departed family members and friends, and attend it as a family.

The fear of the Lord is glory and exultation, and gladness and a crown of rejoicing.
—Sirach 1:11

notes

_____

_____

_____

_____

_____

_____

The Trumpet Shall Sound—The End of the World

Lesson Focus | One day, at the end of time, Jesus will come again to earth in great glory. Then every soul who has ever lived will participate in the General Judgment. All will know who is just and unust; the bodies and souls of all will be reunited, with the just receiving a beautiful, glorified body; and Christ's righteousness and goodness will be made clear. His plan for each human soul, as well as his justice will be shown to be perfect.

1 | begin

- Pray the Glory Be with your child.
- Find online an image of Michelangelo's or Fra Angelico's painting of the Last Judgment. Have your child look carefully at it and describe to you all that he sees.
- Read Mark 13:34–37 aloud.

2 | summarize

Summarize this week's lesson for your child:

Example: *At the end of time, Jesus will come again, and his judgment on every single soul will be made known to all, as will the rightness and justness of his judgment.*

3 | review

Review this week's lesson by asking your child the following questions:

1. Describe the five attributes of the Resurrected Body. (*1. Lucid—beautiful and perfect; 2. Agile—moves through space at the speed of thought; 3. Impassable—incapable of suffering; 4. Immortal—will not die; 5. Spiritual—the will rules the body perfectly.*)
2. What is the Second Coming? (*The event in which Jesus will come to earth at the end of time and appear with power and glory as the King and judge of the world.*)
3. What will happen in the General Judgment? (*All men who have ever lived will be judged, and our deeds and the Lord's judgment will be made known to all, as will God's wisdom and mercy.*)
4. At the General Judgment, what will everyone know about Jesus? (*That he is Lord and God and all his judgments are right and just.*)
5. What is the resurrection of the body? (*After death, our bodies will be transformed by God and reunited with our souls to share in the eternal reward or punishment we have merited.*)

References

- Student Textbook: Chapter 26, pp. 168–71

- Sacred Scripture: Mt 7:13–14; Mk 13:5–37; Lk 21:8–36; Acts 1:1–11; 2 Pet 3:10; Rev 21—22

- *Catechism of the Catholic Church*: 675–82, 988–1004, 1023–57, 2548–50

4 | apply

Help your child apply this week's lesson by asking the following questions:

1. Whose judgment should we care about more—God's or that of the people we know? Why?
2. Whose judgment do you care about more? How do you show this in your actions?
3. What would you like to change about the way you live your life in preparation for the General Judgment?

5 | conclude

- With your child, pray the Our Father.

6 | follow up

During the week, do at least one of the following activities with your child:

1. Memorize 2 Timothy 4:7–8.
2. After school, visit your parish to light a candle and pray for a departed loved one.
3. As a family, say the Prayer to Saint Joseph for a Happy Death (see Appendix).

I have fought the good fight, I have finished the race, I have kept the faith. From now on there is laid up for me the crown of righteousness, which the Lord, the righteous judge, will award to me on that Day, and not only to me but also to all who have loved his appearing.
—2 Timothy 4:7–8

notes

_____

_____

_____

_____

_____

_____

_____

Appendix

The Sign of the Cross

In the name of the Father and of the Son and of the Holy Spirit. *Amen.*

Our Father

Our Father who art in heaven, hallowed be thy name. Thy kingdom come. Thy will be done on earth, as it is in heaven. Give us this day our daily bread, and forgive us our trespasses, as we forgive those who trespass against us, and lead us not into temptation, but deliver us from evil. *Amen.*

Hail Mary

Hail Mary, full of grace, the Lord is with thee. Blessed art thou among women, and blessed is the fruit of thy womb, Jesus. Holy Mary, Mother of God, pray for us sinners now and at the hour of our death. *Amen.*

Glory Be

Glory be to the Father and to the Son and to the Holy Spirit, as it was in the beginning, is now, and ever shall be world without end. *Amen.*

Apostles' Creed

I believe in God, the Father almighty, Creator of heaven and earth, and in Jesus Christ, his only Son, our Lord, who was conceived by the Holy Spirit, born of the Virgin Mary, suffered under Pontius Pilate, was crucified, died, and was buried; he descended into hell; on the third day he rose again from the dead; he ascended into heaven and is seated at the right hand of God the Father almighty; from there he will come to judge the living and the dead. I believe in the Holy Spirit, the holy catholic Church, the communion of saints, the forgiveness of sins, the resurrection of the body, and life everlasting. *Amen.*

Morning Offering

O Jesus, through the Immaculate Heart of Mary, I offer you my prayers, works, joys, and sufferings of this day, in union with the Holy Sacrifice of the Mass throughout the world. I offer them for all the intentions of your Sacred Heart: the salvation of souls, reparation for sin, the reunion of all Christians. I offer them for the intentions of our bishops and of all apostles of prayer, and in particular for those recommended by our Holy Father this month. *Amen.*

Prayer to the Holy Trinity

Glory be to the Father, who by his almighty power and love created me, making me in the image and likeness of God. Glory be to the Son, who by his Precious Blood delivered me from hell and opened for me the gates of heaven. Glory be to the Holy Spirit, who has sanctified me in the Sacrament of Baptism and continues to sanctify me by the graces I receive daily from his bounty. Glory be to the three adorable Persons of the Holy Trinity, now and forever. *Amen.*

Come, Holy Spirit

Come, Holy Spirit, fill the hearts of your faithful and kindle in them the fire of your love. Send forth your Spirit and they shall be created. And you shall renew the face of the earth.

O God, who by the light of the Holy Spirit did instruct the hearts of the faithful, grant that by the same Holy Spirit we may be truly wise and ever enjoy his consolations. Through Christ our Lord. *Amen.*

Holy Spirit Prayer (Saint Augustine)

Breathe in me, O Holy Spirit, that my thoughts may all be holy. Act in me, O Holy Spirit, that my work, too, may be holy. Draw my heart, O Holy Spirit, that I love only what is holy. Strengthen me, O Holy Spirit, to defend all that is holy. Guard me, then, O Holy Spirit, that I may always be holy. *Amen.*

Act of Faith

O my God, I firmly believe that you are one God in three Divine Persons: Father, Son, and Holy Spirit. I believe that your divine Son became man and died for our sins, and that he will come to judge the living and the dead. I believe these and all the truths that the Holy Catholic Church teaches, because you have revealed them, who can neither deceive nor be deceived.

Act of Hope

O Lord God, I hope by your grace for the pardon of all my sins and after life here to gain eternal happiness because you have promised it who are infinitely powerful, faithful, kind, and merciful. In this hope I intend to live and die. *Amen.*

Act of Love

O Lord God, I love you above all things and I love my neighbor for your sake because you are the highest, infinite, and perfect good, worthy of all my love. In this love I intend to live and die. *Amen.*

Act of Contrition

O my God, I am heartily sorry for having offended you. I detest all my sins because of your just punishments, but most of all because they offend you, my God, who are all good and deserving of all my love. I firmly resolve, with the help of your grace, to confess my sins, to do penance, and to amend my life. *Amen.*

Spiritual Communion

My Jesus, as I cannot receive you now in the Most Holy Blessed Sacrament, I ask you to come into my heart and make it like your heart. *Amen.*

Act of Thanksgiving

From the depths of my heart I thank you, dear Lord, for your infinite kindness in coming to me. How good you are to me! With your most holy Mother and all the angels, I praise your mercy and generosity toward me, a poor sinner. I thank you for nourishing my soul with your sacred Body and Precious Blood. I will try to show my gratitude to you in the Sacrament of your love, by obedience to your holy commandments, by fidelity to my duties, by kindness to my neighbor, and by an earnest endeavor to become more like you in my daily conduct. *Amen.*

Anima Christi

Soul of Christ, sanctify me.
Body of Christ, save me.
Blood of Christ, inebriate me.
Water from the side of Christ, wash me.
Passion of Christ, strengthen me.
O good Jesus, hear me.
Within thy wounds hide me.
Suffer me not to be separated from thee.
From the malicious enemy defend me.
In the hour of my death call me
And bid me come unto thee,
That with thy saints I may praise thee
For ever and ever. *Amen.*

Prayer of Abandonment

Father, I abandon myself into your hands; do with me what you will. Whatever you may do, I thank you: I am ready for all, I accept all. Let only your will be done in me, and in all your creatures. I wish no more than this, O Lord.

Into your hands I commend my soul; I offer it to you with all the love of my heart, for I love you, Lord, and so need to give myself, to surrender myself into your hands, without reserve, and with boundless confidence, for you are my Father. *Amen.*

Prayer to the Sacred Heart of Jesus

O most Sacred Heart of Jesus, fountain of every blessing, I adore you, I love you, and with lively sorrow for my sins, I offer you this poor heart of mine. Make me humble, patient, pure, and wholly obedient to your will. Grant, good Jesus, that I may live in you and for you. Protect me in the midst of danger. Comfort me in my afflictions. Give me health of body, assistance in my temporal needs, your blessing on all that I do, and the grace of a holy death. *Amen.*

Hail, Holy Queen

Hail, Holy Queen, Mother of Mercy,
Hail our life, our sweetness, and our hope!
To thee do we cry, poor banished children of Eve.
To thee do we send up our sighs, mourning and weeping in this valley of tears!
Turn, then, most gracious Advocate,
thine eyes of mercy toward us,
and after this, our exile,
show unto us the blessed fruit of thy womb, Jesus.
O clement, O loving,
O sweet Virgin Mary.

Memorare

Remember, O most gracious Virgin Mary, that never was it known that anyone who fled to thy protection, implored thy help, or sought thy intercession was left unaided. Inspired with this confidence, I fly unto thee, O Virgin of Virgins, my Mother; to thee do I come, before thee I stand, sinful and sorrowful. O Mother of the Word Incarnate, despise not my petitions, but in thy mercy hear and answer me. *Amen.*

Prayer of Consecration to Mary

My queen and my Mother, I give myself entirely to you; and to show my devotion to you, I consecrate to you this day my eyes, my ears, my mouth, my heart, my whole being without reserve. Wherefore, good Mother, as I am your own, keep me, guard me, as your property and possession. *Amen.*

The Prayer to My Guardian Angel

Angel of God, my guardian dear, to whom God's love commits me here, ever this day be at my side, to light and guard, to rule and guide. *Amen.*

The Prayer to Saint Michael

Saint Michael the Archangel, defend us in battle. Be our protection against the wickedness and snares of the devil. May God rebuke him, we humbly pray, and do thou, O prince of the heavenly host, by the power of God, thrust into hell Satan and all the evil spirits who prowl about the world seeking the ruin of souls. *Amen.*

Grace Before Meals

Bless us, O Lord, and these thy gifts, which we are about to receive from thy bounty. Through Christ our Lord. *Amen.*

Prayer for the Faithful Departed

Eternal rest grant unto them, O Lord, and let perpetual light shine upon them.
May the souls of the faithful departed, through the mercy of God, rest in peace. *Amen.*

Prayer to Saint Joseph

Gracious Saint Joseph, protect me and my family from all evil as you did the Holy Family. Kindly keep us ever united in the love of Christ, ever fervent in imitation of the virtues of our Blessed Lady, your sinless spouse, and always faithful in devotion to you. *Amen.*

Prayer to Saint Joseph for a Happy Death

Dear Saint Joseph, accept the offering I make to you. Be my father, protector, and guide in the way of salvation. Obtain for me purity of heart and a love for the spiritual life. After your example, let all my actions be directed to the greater glory of God, in union with the Divine Heart of Jesus, the Immaculate Heart of Mary, and your own paternal heart. Finally, pray for me that I may share in the peace and joy of your holy death. *Amen.*

Prayer of Saint Patrick's Breastplate

I bind unto myself today the strong name of the Blessed Trinity, by invocation of the same, the three in one and one in three.

I bind this day to me forever, by power of faith, Christ's Incarnation; his baptism in the Jordan River; his death on the Cross for my salvation; his bursting from the spicèd tomb; his riding up the heavenly way; his coming at the day of doom; I bind unto myself today.

I bind unto myself the power of the great love of the cherubim; the sweet "well done" in judgment hour, the service of the seraphim, confessors' faith, Apostles' word, the patriarchs' prayers, the prophets' scrolls, all good deeds done unto the Lord, and purity of virgin souls.

I bind unto myself today the virtues of the starlit heaven, the glorious sun's life-giving ray, the whiteness of the moon at even, the flashing of the lightning free, the whirling wind's tempestuous shocks, the stable earth, the deep salt sea, around the old eternal rocks.

I bind unto myself today the power of God to hold and lead, his eye to watch, his might to stay, his ear to hearken to my need. The wisdom of my God to teach, his hand to guide, his shield to ward, the word of God to give me speech, his heavenly host to be my guard.

Against the demon snares of sin, the vice that gives temptation force, the natural lusts that war within, the hostile men that mar my course; or few or many, far or nigh, in every place and in all hours, against their fierce hostility, I bind to me these holy powers.

Against all Satan's spells and wiles, against false words of heresy, against the knowledge that defiles, against the heart's idolatry, against the wizard's evil craft, against the death wound and the burning, the choking wave and the poisoned shaft, protect me, Christ, till thy returning.

Christ be with me, Christ within me, Christ behind me, Christ before me, Christ beside me, Christ to win me, Christ to comfort and restore me. Christ beneath me, Christ above me, Christ in quiet, Christ in danger, Christ in hearts of all that love me, Christ in mouth of friend and stranger.

I bind unto myself the name, the strong name of the Blessed Trinity; by invocation of the same. The three in one, and one in three, of whom all nature hath creation, eternal Father, Spirit, Word: praise to the Lord of my salvation; salvation is of Christ the Lord. *Amen.*

Prayer of Saint Francis

Lord, make me an instrument of your peace. Where there is hatred, let me sow love; where there is injury, pardon; where there is doubt, faith; where there is despair, hope; where there is darkness, light; and where there is sadness, joy.

O Divine Master, grant that I may not so much seek to be consoled as to console; to be understood as to understand; to be loved as to love. For it is in giving that we receive; it is in pardoning that we are pardoned; and it is in dying that we are born to eternal life. *Amen.*

Prayer for the Laity (Blessed John Paul II)

O Virgin Mother, guide us and sustain us so that we might always live as true sons and daughters of the Church of your Son. Enable us to do our part in helping to establish on earth the civilization of truth and love as God wills it for his glory. *Amen.*

Saint Teresa's Bookmark (Saint Teresa of Avila)

Let nothing trouble you; let nothing frighten you. All things are passing; God never changes. Patience obtains all things. He who possesses God lacks nothing: God alone suffices.

Litany of Loreto

V. Lord, have mercy.

R. Christ, have mercy.

V. Lord, have mercy. Christ hear us.

R. Christ, graciously hear us.

God the Father of heaven, **have mercy on us.**

God the Son, Redeemer of the world, **have mercy on us.**

God the Holy Spirit, **have mercy on us.**

Holy Trinity, one God, **have mercy on us.**

Holy Mary, **pray for us.**

Holy Mother of God, **pray for us.**

Holy Virgin of virgins, **[etc.]**

Mother of Christ,

Mother of divine grace,

Mother most pure,

Mother most chaste,

Mother inviolate,

Mother undefiled,

Mother most amiable,

Mother most admirable,

Mother of good counsel,

Mother of the Church,

Mother of our Creator,

Mother of our Savior,

Virgin most prudent,

Virgin most venerable,

Virgin most renowned,

Virgin most powerful,

Virgin most merciful,

Virgin most faithful,

Mirror of justice,

Seat of wisdom,

Cause of our joy,

Spiritual vessel,

Vessel of honor,

Singular vessel of devotion,

Mystical rose,

Tower of David,

Tower of ivory,

House of gold,

Ark of the covenant,

Gate of heaven,

Morning star,

Health of the sick,

Refuge of sinners,

Comforter of the afflicted,

Help of Christians,

Queen of Angels,

Queen of Patriarchs,

Queen of Prophets,

Queen of Apostles,

Queen of Martyrs,

Queen of Confessors,

Queen of Virgins,

Queen of all Saints,

Queen conceived without Original Sin,

Queen assumed into heaven,

Queen of the most holy Rosary,

Queen of families,

Queen of peace,

V. Lamb of God, who takes away the sins of the world,

R. Spare us, O Lord.

V. Lamb of God, who takes away the sins of the world,

R. Graciously hear us, O Lord.

V. Lamb of God, who takes away the sins of the world,

R. Have mercy on us.

V. Pray for us, O holy Mother of God.

R. That we may be made worthy of the promises of Christ.

Let us pray: Grant, we beseech thee, O Lord God, unto us they servants, that we may rejoice in continual health of mind and body; and, by the glorious intercession of blessed Mary, ever virgin, may be delivered from present sadness, and enter into the joy of thine eternal gladness. Through Christ our Lord. Amen.

The Mysteries of the Rosary

The Joyful Mysteries

1. The Annunciation (Lk 1:26–38)
2. The Visitation (Lk 1:39–56)
3. The Nativity (Lk 2:1–21)
4. The Presentation (Lk 2:22–38)
5. The Finding in the Temple (Lk 2:41–52)

The Luminous Mysteries

1. The Baptism of Christ in the Jordan (Mt 3:13–16)
2. The Wedding Feast at Cana (Jn 2:1–11)
3. The Proclamation of the Kingdom of God (Mk 1:14–15)
4. The Transfiguration of Our Lord (Mt 17:1–8)
5. The Institution of the Eucharist (Mt 26)

The Sorrowful Mysteries

1. The Agony in the Garden (Mt 26:36–56)
2. The Scourging at the Pillar (Mt 27:26)
3. The Crowning with Thorns (Mt 27:27–31)
4. The Carrying of the Cross (Mt 27:32)
5. The Crucifixion (Mt 27:33–56)

The Glorious Mysteries

1. The Resurrection (Jn 20:1–29)
2. The Ascension (Lk 24:36–53)
3. The Descent of the Holy Spirit (Acts 2:1–41)
4. The Assumption (Rev 11:19)
5. The Coronation (Rev 12:1)

The Stations of the Cross

1. Jesus is condemned to death
2. Jesus carries his cross
3. Jesus falls the first time
4. Jesus meets his Mother
5. Jesus is helped by Simon of Cyrene
6. Veronica wipes the face of Jesus
7. Jesus falls a second time
8. Jesus speaks to the women
9. Jesus falls a third time
10. Jesus is stripped of his clothes
11. Jesus is nailed to the cross
12. Jesus dies on the cross
13. Jesus is taken down from the cross
14. Jesus is placed in the tomb

Divine Mercy Chaplet

1. Begin with the Sign of the Cross, then pray one Our Father, one Hail Mary, and the Apostles' Creed.

2. On the Our Father beads say the following:
   "Eternal Father, I offer you the Body and Blood, Soul, and Divinity of your dearly beloved Son, our Lord Jesus Christ, in atonement for our sins and those of the whole world."

3. On each Hail Mary bead say the following:
   "For the sake of his sorrowful Passion, have mercy on us and on the whole world." (Repeat steps 2 and 3 for all five decades.)

4. Say (three times):
   "Holy God, Holy Mighty One, Holy Immortal One, have mercy on us and on the whole world."

5. Conclude with the Sign of the Cross.

Renewal of Baptismal Promises

V. Do you renounce Satan?

R. I do.

V. And all his works?

R. I do.

V. And all his empty show?

R. I do.

V. Do you believe in God,
   the Father almighty,
   Creator of heaven and earth?

R. I do.

V. Do you believe in Jesus Christ, his only Son, our Lord,
   who was born of the Virgin Mary,
   suffered death and was buried,
   rose again from the dead
   and is seated at the right hand of the Father?

R. I do.

V. Do you believe in the Holy Spirit,
   the holy Catholic Church,
   the communion of saints,
   the forgiveness of sins,
   the resurrection of the body,
   and life everlasting?

R. I do.

V. And may almighty God, the Father of our Lord Jesus Christ,
   who has given us new birth by water and the Holy Spirit

and bestowed on us forgiveness of our sins,
keep us by his grace,
in Christ Jesus our Lord,
for eternal life.

R. Amen.

Latin Lines

Sign of the Cross
In the name of the Father and of the Son and of the Holy Spirit. **Amen.**

> In nomine Patris et Filii et Spiritus Sancti. **Amen.**

Confiteor
I confess to almighty God and to you, my brothers and sisters, that I have greatly sinned, in my thoughts and in my words, in what I have done and in what I have failed to do; through my fault, through my fault, through my most grievous fault; therefore I ask blessed Mary ever-Virgin, all the Angels and Saints, and you, my brothers and sisters, to pray for me to the Lord our God.

> Confiteor Deo omnipotenti et vobis, fratres, quia peccavi nimis cogitatione, verbo, opere et omissione: mea culpa, mea culpa, mea maxima culpa. Ideo precor beatam Mariam semper Virginem, omnes Angelos et Sanctos, et vos, fratres, orare pro me ad Dominum Deum nostrum.

Greek Lines

Confiteor
Lord, have mercy. Christ, have mercy. Lord, have mercy.

> Kyrie, eleison. Christe, eleison. Kyrie, eleison.

The Ten Commandments
1. I am the LORD your God; you shall not have other gods before me.
2. You shall not take the name of the LORD your God in vain.
3. Remember to keep holy the LORD's day.
4. Honor your father and mother.
5. You shall not kill.
6. You shall not commit adultery.
7. You shall not steal.

Seven Gifts of the Holy Spirit
1. Wisdom
2. Understanding
3. Counsel (right judgment)
4. Fortitude (courage)
5. Knowledge
6. Piety
7. Fear of the Lord
8. You shall not bear false witness against your neighbor.
9. You shall not covet your neighbor's wife.
10. You shall not covet your neighbor's goods.

Fruits of the Holy Spirit
1. Charity (or love)
2. Joy
3. Peace
4. Patience
5. Kindness
6. Goodness
7. Long-suffering
8. Mildness
9. Faith
10. Modesty
11. Continence
12. Chastity

The Corporal Works of Mercy
1. Feed the hungry
2. Give drink to the thirsty
3. Clothe the naked
4. Visit the imprisoned
5. Shelter the homeless
6. Visit the sick
7. Bury the dead

The Spiritual Works of Mercy
1. Admonish the sinner
2. Instruct the ignorant
3. Counsel the doubtful
4. Comfort the sorrowful
5. Bear wrongs patiently
6. Forgive all injuries
7. Pray for the living and the dead

Image Credits